THE NETHERLANDS
Practical Commercial Law

WILLEM A HOYNG
JULIE A ROELVINK
FRANCINE M SCHLINGMANN
De Brauw Blackstone Westbroek

LONGMAN

© Longman Group Ltd 1992

Published by
Longman Law, Tax and Finance
Longman Group UK Ltd
21–27 Lamb's Conduit Street
London WC1N 3NJ

Associated offices
Australia, Hong Kong, Malaysia, Singapore, USA

ISBN 0 85121 777 X

Typeset by Servis Filmsetting Ltd, Manchester

Printed and bound in Great Britain by Biddles Ltd, Guildford,
Surrey

CONTENTS

Chapter Eight: Insolvency

PREFACE

In this book we endeavour to provide a concise and practical, but nevertheless thorough, survey of the main areas of commercial law in the Netherlands. Practising as Dutch lawyers in the London office of De Brauw Blackstone Westbroek, we have the benefit of our daily experience with foreign (especially UK based) clients and their questions on the legal aspects of doing business in the Netherlands.

Inevitably, not all subjects in the areas dealt with can be covered. We have also decided not to include a chapter on taxes in the Netherlands, as this would have gone beyond the scope of this book. For Dutch taxation, we may refer to another Longman publication: *Corporate Taxation in EC Countries* (edited by Jean-Marc Tirard).

By necessity the survey is of a general nature and does not constitute legal advice.

The manuscript was finalised on 1 March 1992. To the extent possible, expected changes in the law which will come into force in the course of 1992 are dealt with.

We would like to thank those of our colleagues in the firm who have commented on the manuscript. Special thanks should go to Alexandra Oud for the meticulous work she did on the typing of the manuscript.

Professor Willem Hoyng
Julie Roelvink
Francine Schlingmann
London, May 1992

INTRODUCTION

SOURCES OF DUTCH LAW

STATUTES

The Dutch legal system is a civil law system. Statutes are the main source of law. As a result of the French occupation of the Netherlands in the early nineteenth century, codification has developed on the basis of the French 'Codes'.

The main parts of the Dutch codification are:
(1) the Civil Code (*Burgerlijk Wetboek*);
(2) the Commercial Code (*Wetboek van Koophandel*);
(3) the Criminal Code (*Wetboek van Strafrecht*);
(4) the Code of Civil Procedure (*Wetboek van Burgerlijke Rechtsvordering*);
(5) the Code of Criminal Procedure (*Wetboek van Strafvordering*).

CASE LAW

In addition to statutes, case law is also an important source of law. Decisions by the courts, especially decisions by the Supreme Court of the Netherlands, are important for the interpretation of provisions in the codes and statutes. This interpretation sometimes comes down to the creation of new rules of law.

A Dutch court is not bound by previous decisions of other courts nor by its own previous decisions. However, lower courts normally follow decisions of higher courts, and especially those of the Supreme Court.

TREATIES

Another important source of law is formed by treaties. In as far as treaties contain rules for the contracting parties, they form a source of international law. Treaties may also contain so-called 'self executing' provisions. Such provisions, which have direct effect, are a source of national law. If a provision of a treaty has direct effect, it even prevails over provisions in codes and statutes. A very important example of a treaty that contains self-executing provisions is the EC Treaty.

THE NEW CIVIL CODE

Since 1947 the Civil Code has been subject to a complete revision. In 1970 the first stage of this revision was completed upon the coming into force of Book 1 on family law. In 1976 Book 2 came into force. Book 2 contains the law on legal entities and will be extensively dealt with in the chapter on business structures. On 1 January 1992 Books 3, 5 and 6, containing in broad terms the law of contract, the law of tort and the law relating to ownership and other rights *in rem*, came into force. Four parts of Book 7, which deals with specific types of contracts, also became effective on 1 January 1992. These parts relate to purchase and sale agreements, mandate (*lastgeving*), custodianship (*bewaarneming*) and surety (*borgtocht*). A new Book 4 on the law of inheritance and the remaining parts of Book 7, such as the part on employment agreements, will come into force at a later date.

Part of the revision is also to integrate the provisions of the present Commercial Code into the New Civil Code. This has already partly been achieved by the new Book 8, which became effective on 1 April 1991. This concerns the law of transport.

Other subjects which are presently dealt with in the Commercial Code, such as insurance and agency, will be included in Book 7.

COURT SYSTEM

GENERAL

Without prejudice to the jurisdiction of special courts in respect of certain matters specified in the law, the judicial power in civil and criminal matters is exercised by:

(1) the Cantonal Courts (*Kantongerechten*);
(2) the District Courts (*Arrondissementsrechtbanken*);
(3) the Courts of Appeal (*Gerechtshoven*); and
(4) the Supreme Court of the Netherlands (*Hoge Raad der*

Nederlanden; further referred to as 'Supreme Court').
With a view to the scope of this book, jurisdiction in criminal matters will not be further dealt with.

CANTONAL COURTS

There are 62 Cantonal Courts. The Cantonal Court, consisting of one judge, deals, in first instance, with the following matters:

(1)   personal claims that do not exceed Dfl5,000; there is no appeal if the claim does not exceed Dfl2,500;
(2)   matters (irrespective of the amount of the claim) relating to:
    (a)   an employment agreement;
    (b)   an agency agreement;
    (c)   a collective bargaining agreement;
    (d)   a hire-purchase agreement;
    (e)   a tenancy agreement;
    there is no appeal if the claim does not exceed Dfl2,500;
(3)   claims in connection with certain works council matters (see section **1.11**);
(4)   certain other matters which for the purpose of this book are less important.

DISTRICT COURTS

There are 19 District Courts. They have jurisdiction in first instance in respect of all matters that are not specifically submitted to the jurisdiction of other courts. The District Courts also deal with appeals from Cantonal Court decisions. It depends on the nature and/or the 'importance' of a matter whether it is decided by one judge or three judges.

THE PRESIDENT OF THE DISTRICT COURT FOR PRELIMINARY RELIEF

In all cases in which it is necessary to obtain immediate relief, it is possible to initiate what we will refer to as 'preliminary relief proceedings' (*kort geding*) before the president of the District Court. Such proceedings are by comparison to 'normal' proceedings fairly informal. Relief can be obtained in a very short period of time, sometimes within a few hours. Although the decision of the president is preliminary to be followed by normal proceedings, parties often decide to refrain from such normal proceedings.

Relief in preliminary proceedings usually takes the form of an injunction against the defendant or an order to the defendant to do something.

COURTS OF APPEAL

There are five Courts of Appeal. Their most important task is to deal with appeals from District Court decisions and decisions of presidents of the District Courts in preliminary relief proceedings (see above). They sit with three judges.

Each Court of Appeal has a special tax division that deals with appeals (from first instance decisions of inspectors of taxes) in tax matters.

The Court of Appeal in Amsterdam has a special Enterprise Division (*Ondernemingskamer*) which deals, in first instance, with requests to order an inquiry (see section **1.9.3**) and with matters relating to annual accounts (see section **1.10.3**). The Enterprise Division also deals with appeals from decisions of the District Courts in certain shareholders' disputes (see section **1.9.2**). The Enterprise Division sits with three members of the judiciary and two experts.

The Court of Appeal in Arnhem has a special division dealing with appeals from Cantonal Court decisions in matters relating to leases of land.

SUPREME COURT

The most important task of the Supreme Court is to decide on appeals in cassation (*cassatie*) mainly from appeal decisions of District Courts and Courts of Appeal. The Supreme Court will only decide on questions of law and not on the facts of the matter.

SPECIAL COURTS

Special courts and procedures exist for:
(1)   complaints about decisions made by central government bodies and by provincial, municipal and other non-central government authorities;
(2)   social security matters;

(3)   matters regarding the relation between central or local government authorities and civil servants; and
(4)   matters regarding certain special rules and regulations for trade and industry.

ARBITRATION

The Code of Civil Procedure contains separate rules which apply to any arbitration conducted in the Netherlands, irrespective of the nationality of the parties. The rules relate to, *inter alia*, the agreement to settle disputes by arbitration, the appointment of arbitrators, the manner in which the proceedings are conducted, the arbitral award and its execution.

Apart from specialised arbitration institutes, there is also an institute for arbitration that may deal with any type of disputes. This is the Netherlands Arbitration Institute (*Nederlands Arbitrage Instituut*) which has adopted its own rules.

In connection with foreign arbitral awards, it is important to note that the Netherlands is party to the 1958 New York Convention on the recognition and enforcement of foreign arbitral awards.

THE LEGAL PROFESSIONS

GENERAL

In this paragraph the following legal professions will be described:
(1)   the *advocaat*;
(2)   the *notaris*;
(3)   the in-house company lawyer;
(4)   the tax adviser; and
(5)   the bailiff.

THE *ADVOCAAT*

An *advocaat* (further referred to as 'advocate') may be compared to an American attorney at law who has been admitted to the bar. There is no distinction between barristers and solicitors, as in England. An advocate gives advice to his clients and may also represent them in court.

ADMISSION

To be admitted to the bar of the District Court in the region within which the advocate has his office, certain requirements must be met. The advocate is admitted as such if he has obtained a university degree in Dutch law. This is the degree of *Meester in de rechten*, confusingly abbreviated to 'Mr'. He is sworn in by the relevant District Court. The admission takes place conditionally if the applicant cannot produce evidence that he has passed the professional education exams. In practice, the professional education course is usually followed during the first year of practice. Once the relevant exams have been passed and the required evidence is produced within three years after conditional admission the admission becomes final.

STAGE

During the first three years of his practice the advocate is supervised by an experienced advocate. This three-year period is called *stage*. It cannot be compared to the two years of 'articles' in an English firm of solicitors. Effectively, the only restriction is that a *stagiaire* cannot set up his own independent practice.

RIGHT OF AUDIENCE

Advocates have right of audience in all courts in the Netherlands, the European Court of Justice and the Benelux Court of Justice. Before the Supreme Court representation by Supreme Court advocates (advocates admitted to the bar of the district court in the Hague) is required.

To file written statements with a District Court other than the one to which he is admitted, the assistance of a *procureur*, admitted to the relevant District Court, is required. The assistance rendered by the *procureur* is just a formality: he signs the statements, the advocate handles the case. Nearly all advocates are also *procureur* in their district.

On the basis of the EC Directive of 22 March 1977 (Official Journal of the EC L78 of 26 March 1977) 'visiting' EC lawyers (persons who have been admitted to the bar in an EC Member State) may render their professional services in the Netherlands; they are subject to the same rules and regulations as lawyers who have been admitted to the Dutch Bar as advocates. If a 'visiting' EC lawyer provides services to a client in a matter in which Dutch law prescribes court representation by an advocate (or *procureur*) the 'visiting' lawyer *must* work with an advocate admitted to the Dutch Bar.

ORGANISATION

An advocate is a member of both the local bar association in his court district and of the Dutch Bar Association (*Nederlandse Orde van Advocaten*). Advocates must comply with the Rules of Conduct (*Gedragsregels*) and various other rules and regulations issued by the Dutch Bar Association. There is a special system of disciplinary jurisdiction.

LAW FIRMS

Most advocates practise within partnership firms. In recent years, Dutch law firms have—particularly as a result of mergers— become much bigger than they used to be. In a number of firms there are also *notarissen*, civil law notaries, whose profession will be discussed below.

THE *NOTARIS*

The *notaris* or civil law notary cannot be compared to the notary public in countries with an Anglo-Saxon legal system. The civil law notary mainly deals with conveyancing, (shipping) mortgages, incorporation of companies and establishment of foundations and (co-operative) associations, wills and marriage settlements, for which notarial deeds are required. The civil law notary is usually 'neutral' and therefore does not act on behalf of one particular party. He may, however, act as legal adviser to one party, especially when the other has its own legal adviser, provided he makes this clear to all parties involved.

APPOINTMENT

The civil law notary is appointed by the Queen. The requirements for appointment are:
(1)   having Dutch nationality;
(2)   being 25 years of age but younger than 65;

(3) being candidate civil law notary (*kandidaat-notaris*); this means having obtained a university degree in Dutch notarial law; and

(4) having worked at one or more notary offices as a candidate for at least three years.

The number of seats (*standplaatsen*) for civil law notaries is limited and it often takes many years before a candidate is appointed as civil law notary.

ORGANISATION AND SUPERVISION

Virtually all civil law notaries are members of the Royal Association of Civil Law Notaries (*Koninklijke Notariële Broederschap*), which has a division in each of the 19 court districts.

Supervision of (candidate) civil law notaries is exercised by Chambers of Supervision (*Kamers van Toezicht*) in the different court districts. The Chambers of Supervision may hear complaints about (candidate) civil law notaries. It may also take certain disciplinary measures.

THE IN-HOUSE COMPANY LAWYER

A large number of Dutch companies employ in-house lawyers. Most in-house company lawyers are members of the Association of Company Lawyers (*Nederlands Genootschap van Bedrijfsjuristen*).

Company lawyers do not have right of audience in the courts where representation by an advocate is mandatory.

THE TAX ADVISER

Unlike the professions of advocate and civil law notary, the profession of tax adviser is not protected by law. There are no statutory rules or regulations which govern the profession of tax adviser or tax consultant. Any person can hold himself out as such, regardless of whether he has any academic or other relevant qualifications.

There are, however, two professional organisations that apply their own qualification requirements and have their own membership rules and regulations. Those two organisations are:

(1) the Dutch Order of Tax Advisers (*Nederlandse Orde van Belastingadviseurs*); and

(2)   the Dutch Federation of Tax Consultants (*Nederlandse
      Federatie van Belastingconsulenten*).

   Both organisations have issued rules of conduct that have to
be observed by the members and that are similar to those of other
professional organisations.

THE BAILIFF

   Bailiffs (*deurwaarders*) are appointed by the Queen. They are
public officials. Their public duties are:

(1)   the performance of certain official tasks on the instructions
      of parties or their *procureurs* in civil proceedings such as
      issuing notices or writs of summons and other official
      documents;
(2)   the performance of certain tasks in the courts such as calling
      the cases dealt with and maintaining the order.

Apart from their public tasks, bailiffs also render legal services
and sometimes represent parties in Cantonal Court proceedings.
In Cantonal Court proceedings there is no mandatory court
representation (by advocates).

   Disciplinary supervision of bailiffs is exercised by the
Minister of Justice and the Cantonal Courts.

INSTITUTIONS RELEVANT TO THE BUSINESS COMMUNITY

CHAMBERS OF COMMERCE AND INDUSTRY

   At present there are 37 Chambers of Commerce and
Industry (*Kamers van Koophandel en Fabrieken*), each of which
covers a particular district.

   The general task of the Chambers of Commerce is the
promotion and support of trade and industry within their
districts.

   In addition, they have special duties and responsibilities set
out in various acts such as the Trade Register Act (*Handelsregister-
wet*). The Chambers of Commerce maintain the trade register
which contains information on business enterprises. This information is available for inspection by the public. The information
must be provided to the Chamber of Commerce by the owner of
the enterprise or—if the enterprise is run by a legal entity—by its

management. An important feature of the trade register system is that third parties may rely on the information in the trade register, irrespective of whether it is complete and correct. Facts which have not been entered cannot be invoked against third parties who were unaware of them.

THE ACT ON THE TRADE ORGANISATION

On the basis of the Act on the Trade Organisation (*Wet op de Bedrijfsorganisatie*) certain institutions have the authority to issue rules and regulations on (various sectors of) trade and industry. These institutions are:
(1)   the Social and Economic Council (*Sociaal-Economische Raad*);
(2)   the Product Boards (*Productschappen*);
(3)   the Central Trade Boards (*Hoofdbedrijfschappen*) and the Trade Boards (*Bedrijfschappen*).

Product Boards are established for enterprises which have different functions in the production and distribution process of one product or a group of products. (Central) Trade Boards are established for enterprises which have similar functions in a particular industry or trade. The Product and (Central) Trade Boards are managed by representatives of organisations of employers and employees.

THE SOCIAL AND ECONOMIC COUNCIL

With a view to the subject matter of this book it is important to describe the organisation and the main tasks of the Social and Economic Council.
The members of the Council are appointed:
(1)   one third by employers' organisations;
(2)   one third by employees' organisations; and
(3)   one third by the Dutch government.
    Its main tasks are:
(1)   to advise the government on important social and economic matters;
(2)   to supervise the Product and (Central) Trade Boards;
(3)   to administer certain legislation for trade and industry;
(4)   to issue rules and regulations to promote the interests of the business community.

The Council has, for instance, used its regulatory authority in issuing the Merger Code (see section **3.3.2**). For particular matters the Council may establish permanent committees, such as the Committee for Merger Affairs (see section **3.3.2**), as well as *ad hoc* committees.

ENTERPRISE COMMITTEES

On the basis of the Works Council Act, the Social and Economic Council has established committees for various groups of enterprises. These Enterprise Committees (*Bedrijfscommissies*) which consist of representatives of employers' and employees' organisations mediate in certain works council disputes (see section **1.11.5**).

COURT OF APPEAL FOR TRADE AND INDUSTRY

There is a Court of Appeal for Trade and Industry (*College van Beroep voor het Bedrijfsleven*) which hears appeals from decisions by the Social and Economic Council and the Product and (Central) Trade Boards. This court also has jurisdiction in a variety of other matters such as decisions by the Minister of Finance or the Securities Board on the basis of the Act on the supervision of the securities trade (see section **5.1.6**) and the Act on the supervision of investment institutions (see section **5.2.5**).

OTHER ORGANISATIONS

Of course, there are many other organisations which are of importance when looking into Dutch commercial law. They cannot all be listed here, but several of them are mentioned in the following chapters.

1

BUSINESS STRUCTURES

1.1 INTRODUCTION

As most business in the Netherlands is conducted by companies, the two types of Dutch companies, NVs and BVs, will be the main focus of this chapter. First, however, a brief summary of the forms of business organisations available in the Netherlands and of other organisation forms will be provided. The companies, associations and foundations are provided for in Book 2 of the Dutch Civil Code which deals with legal entities (*rechtspersonen*). The rules on partnerships can be found, at present, in the Civil Code (Book 4) and in the Dutch Commercial Code.

A Sole ownership

A natural person may conduct a business. This business must be registered with the trade register. The owner of the business will be liable, with his entire property, for all acts carried out as part of the business.

B Companies

The NV (*naamloze vennootschap*) is a public company with limited liability. The BV (*besloten vennootschap*) is a private company with limited liability. The main differences between the two companies are:

(1) the shares in the NV are in bearer (section **1.3.2**) or in registered form (section **1.3.4**); the shares in the BV are in registered form only;

(2) the minimum issued and paid-up capital of the NV is Dfl 100,000; the BV's minimum capital is presently Dfl 40,000;

(3) the BV must, by statute, restrict the transfer of its shares whereas for the NV such restriction is optional;

(4)   the rules relating to the purchase by the company of shares in its capital and to financial assistance by the company are stricter for an NV than for a BV.

In view of the mandatory restriction on the transfer of its shares, the BV form is particularly suitable for wholly-owned subsidiaries, joint-venture companies and family business. The NV is suitable for larger companies whose shares are or may be listed.

C Partnerships

A partnership under Dutch law can be defined as an agreement whereby two or more parties contribute capital, labour or, for instance, goods, rights or goodwill with the purpose of making a profit and of distributing the profits among the partners. The partners can be individuals or legal entities.

At present, a distinction should be made between:

(1)   *Civil partnership* (*maatschap*). This legal form is mostly used for the conduct of a profession. In the draft for Book 7 of the new Dutch Civil Code, the civil partnership will be divided into 'public partnerships' (*openbare vennootschappen*) and 'silent partnerships' (*stille vennootschappen*). Contrary to all partnerships at present, the public partnership is, in the current draft of Book 7, proposed to have legal personality. The commercial partnership and the limited partnership (see under (2) and (3)) will be forms of public partnerships.

(2)   *Commercial partnership* (*vennootschap onder firma*). This partnership has the object of conducting a business under a collective name. Commercial partnerships must be registered with the trade register, but they do not have to disclose accounts. Unlike the civil partnership, the commercial partnership can be represented by each partner, unless the partnership agreement provides otherwise. Limitations on authority to enter into transactions on behalf of the commercial partnership can only be invoked against third parties if such limitations are filed with the trade register.

Contrary to partners of a civil partnership, each partner of a commercial partnership is, in addition to the partnership itself, severally liable for the obligations of the company arising from contract or statute.

(3)   *Limited partnership* (*commanditaire vennootschap*). This part-

nership is similar to the commercial partnership, but has two types of partners:

(a)　one or more managing (*beherende*) partners who are authorised to act on behalf of the limited partnership and who are severally liable for all obligations of the partnership;

(b)　one or more 'silent' (*commanditaire*) partners who are only liable to the extent of their contribution but cannot act on behalf of the company.

D Associations (*Verenigingen*)

As a general rule, associations cannot distribute profits among their members and are therefore unsuitable as a business structure. There are, however, two types of associations, which may distribute profits amongst their members:

(1)　*The cooperative* (*cooperatie*). The cooperative's object is to provide for certain material needs of its members by the conclusion of agreements with the members in the business it conducts for the benefit of the members, other than insurance agreements; the cooperative is mostly used in the agricultural business.

(2)　*The mutual insurance society* (*onderlinge waarborgmaatschappij*). This society's object is to conclude insurance contracts with its members in the insurance business it conducts for the benefit of its members.

The cooperative and the mutual insurance society must both be established by a notarial deed and registered with the trade register. The liability of members in a cooperative or a mutual insurance society can be limited or excluded. In this case the letters 'BA' (*beperkte aansprakelijkheid* which means 'limited liability') or 'UA' (*uitsluiting van aansprakelijkheid* which means 'exclusion of liability') are placed at the end of its name.

One bank in the Netherlands is a cooperative: Coöperatieve Raiffeissen Boerenleenbank BA (*Rabobank*).

E Foundations (*Stichtingen*)

A foundation is a legal entity with no members. It is established by notarial deed (ie by deed passed before a Dutch civil law notary, see **Introduction**). Its objects do not have to be charitable but they may not include the making of contributions to the founders or the members of its board or directors (or of other bodies).

Contributions to other persons may only be made if these have an idealistic or social purpose.

A separate register of foundations is kept at the Chamber of Commerce.

The administration offices established by Dutch companies in connection with oligarchic or protective measures are usually in the form of a foundation (see section **1.3.1**).

1.2 INCORPORATION OF COMPANIES

1.2.1 INCORPORATION REQUIREMENTS AND PROCEDURE

There are three basic requirements for the incorporation of an NV or BV:

(1) there must be one or more incorporators (founder members) participating in the company's capital;
(2) a notarial deed, containing the articles of association, must be passed;
(3) the Ministry of Justice must have approved the notarial deed before it is executed (the so-called 'statement of no-objection').

Incorporator(s)

The NV or BV can be incorporated by one or more persons. 'Person' includes a legal entity.

Each incorporator must participate in the capital by taking at least one share, unless the incorporation takes place by a deed of legal merger (see section **3.2**).

Other shareholders, not being incorporators, may take the remainder of the minimum share capital required by law (see on minimum capital requirements section **1.4.1**).

Notarial deed

The deed of incorporation must be passed before a Dutch civil law notary (see **Introduction**) and must be in the Dutch language. The incorporator(s) may be represented by a written power of attorney.

The deed of incorporation must contain:

(1) the articles of association of the company (see below);

(2)   the amounts of the issued and paid up share capital;
       the issued share capital has to be specified as to each class of
       shares and as to the amount subscribed by each incorpora-
       tor;
(3)   the name(s) of the first managing director(s) and the first
       supervisory director(s) if the company has a supervisory
       board.

Certain documents relating to the manner in which payment
on the initial share capital is made (see sections **1.4.2** and **1.4.3**),
are attached to the deed of incorporation when the deed is passed.

Articles of association

The articles of association must contain at least the
following information:
(1)   The name of the company. This name must begin or end
       with *Naamloze vennootschap* or *Besloten vennootschap met
       beperkte aansprakelijkheid* (or 'NV' or 'BV').
(2)   The seat of the company. This 'corporate seat' (comparable
       to registered office) must be in the Netherlands. The seat
       does not have to be in the same city or town as the
       company's place of business. The law requires that an NV or
       BV must clearly show its full name and its corporate seat in
       all documents and announcements which it issues or to
       which it is a party.
(3)   The objects of the company. Usually this is a brief
       description of the proposed activities of the company (often
       followed by words such as '... and anything which is
       connected therewith or may be conducive thereto').
       The subject of transgression by the company of its
       objects (*ultra vires*) is discussed below in section **1.6.4.**
(4)   The amount of the authorised share capital and (if there are
       different classes of shares, for each class) the number and
       denomination of the shares.
(5)   The manner in which the company is provisionally managed
       if managing directors are absent or prevented from acting.

The articles of association will also set out the management
structure of the company and the manner in which the company
can be represented. The articles will describe further details such
as capital, transfer of shares and restriction on such transfer,
shareholders' meetings, annual accounts, amendment of the

articles and liquidation of the company.

The articles thus serve an additional purpose of information and guidelines for the persons responsible for managing the company.

Statement of no-objection

The 'statement of no-objection' is the term used for the necessary approval by the Minister of Justice of the proposed deed of incorporation. To obtain a statement of no-objection, a draft of the deed of incorporation must be submitted to the Minister of Justice and an application fee of Dfl 175 must be paid. The application is usually made by the civil law notary on behalf of the incorporator(s).

The Ministry may only refuse the statement if:

(1)   the deed is contrary to public order or the law; or

(2)   considering the intentions or past record of the person(s) who will determine the policy of the company, there is a risk that the company will be used for unlawful purposes or that the company's activities will prejudice its creditors.

In considering the application, the Ministry is guided by its 'Departmental Guidelines' (last edition 1986). These guidelines do not have force of law, but are generally adhered to.

In view of the second possible ground of refusal the Ministry checks the credentials of each incorporator and initial managing director. Each natural person residing in the Netherlands or of Dutch nationality must complete a detailed questionnaire including questions on any previous bankruptcy and on the financing of the initially issued shares and the activities of the company. A foreign natural person not residing in the Netherlands will (*inter alia*) have to submit a letter of good standing issued by a reputable bank. Legal entities acting as incorporator or managing director must also submit information about their business.

The Ministry will furthermore wish to know if the incorporators intend to transfer their shares to third parties or make changes in the managing board within one year of incorporation. If this is the case, the Ministry will require information regarding such third parties or future managing directors.

1.2.2 REGISTRATION OF THE COMPANY

General
The managing director(s) of the newly incorporated NV or BV must have the company registered with the trade register of the Chamber of Commerce and Industry (see **Introduction**) in the district in which the NV or BV has its corporate seat. If the company's principal place of business and the company's corporate seat are in different districts, subject to different Chambers of Commerce and Industry, registration of the company must take place with the trade register of both Chambers.

Details to be registered
The information to be registered includes:
(1)   the name and trade name of the company;
(2)   the corporate seat and principal place of business;
(3)   the objects of the company;
(4)   details of each (or the only) managing director (and supervisory director) of the company and a specimen of their signatures and initials;
(5)   date of appointment of the managing (and supervisory) director(s) and with respect to each (or the only) managing director the scope of his authority to represent the company (see section **1.6.4**);
(6)   the authorised, issued and paid-up share capital;
(7)   a certified copy of the deed of incorporation (upon an amendment of the articles of association a copy of the deed of amendment and the full text of the amended articles of association must be filed).

Liability for non- or incorrect registration
Under Dutch law, the registration of the company is not a condition for the creation of the company. However, the managing director(s) will, in addition to the company itself, be jointly and severally liable for transactions of the company entered into before the initial registration of the company has been duly applied for.
The information filed with the trade register is available for public inspection and can in principle be relied upon. The

company cannot invoke any facts which have not been registered or which have been incorrectly or incompletely registered, against third parties who were unaware of this. For instance, an agreement signed by a managing director is binding upon the company, if the limitations on the authority of the managing director to represent the company (as contained in the articles of association) were not registered and were not known to the other party to the agreement.

Registration of shareholders

If shares in a company have not been fully paid up, the Trade Register Act requires that the names and addresses of the holders of such shares are registered. At present, there is no other requirement to register the names of shareholders. With respect to companies which have only one shareholder this will change soon. Pursuant to the Twelfth EC Company Law Directive (Official Journal 1989 L395/40), an amendment of the Trade Register Act is proposed, which contains a provision requiring all companies with only one shareholder to register the fact that they are solely owned as well as the name of the sole shareholder. The amendment came into force in March 1992.

1.2.3 DEFECTIVE INCORPORATION

The provisions in Book 2 of the Civil Code dealing with the consequences of defective incorporation have been revised. The new provisions which came into force on 1 January 1992 make a distinction between two 'groups' of defects:

(1) If there is no notarial deed or no statement of no-objection (see section **1.2.1**), the company will not come into existence. The company's assets, if there are any, will be liquidated. This takes place in the same manner as the liquidation of a company's assets upon its winding up (see section **1.8.3**). The persons acting as managing directors can be held liable for the debts of the 'non existing' company.

(2) In case of any other defect in the incorporation, the consequence is that the company is wound up (see section **1.8.3**) by the District Court, at the request of any interested party or the public prosecutor.

1.2.4   ACTS OF THE COMPANY BEFORE INCORPORATION

General

The incorporators, or future managing directors, may enter into transactions on behalf of the company before its incorporation has been completed. Such acting on behalf of a company to be incorporated is quite common. Often, the words 'NV io' or 'BV io' ('io' means: 'to be incorporated') are added to the name of the company to be incorporated.

The question arises to what extent the company is bound by legal acts performed in its name before incorporation. Dutch company law provides that the company is bound by legal acts performed in its name before incorporation if (i) the company expressly or implicitly ratifies such acts after its incorporation or (ii) in case of certain specified acts only, if the incorporators bind the company directly in the deed of incorporation.

Binding by deed of incorporation

The company can only be bound directly by deed of incorporation in the following cases:

(1)   the issue of shares;

(2)   the acceptance of payments on shares;

(3)   the appointment of managing directors and supervisory directors; and

(4)   certain transactions described by paragraph 1 of Article 94/ 204 Book 2 Civil Code including payment on shares in kind.

Ratification—liability

In all other transactions the company can only be bound by ratification after incorporation. The term 'legal acts', in the context of the provisions for ratification, does not include tortious acts committed by the incorporators before incorporation. After the incorporation, the company cannot be held liable for such acts.

Until the company has ratified a 'legal act', the persons who performed such legal act before the incorporation are jointly and severally liable for such act. Moreover, if the company does ratify the 'legal act' but breaches its obligations arising from such act, the same persons will be liable for any damages suffered by third parties if they knew or could reasonably have known that the company would breach its obligations. This knowledge is presumed to exist if the company is declared bankrupt within a year after incorporation. The managing director(s) of the company will also be liable in connection with the ratification.

1.3 SHARES

1.3.1 INTRODUCTION

Distinction NV—BV

The most prominent distinction between the NV and BV lies in the type of shares which can be issued and the restriction on the transfer of shares. The shares in the NV are freely transferable unless the articles of association restrict the transfer of shares. In the case of the BV, the articles of association must include provisions restricting the transfer of shares.

The shares in the NV may be registered shares (with or without corresponding share certificates) or bearer shares. The BV can only issue registered shares and cannot issue share certificates.

Special types of shares

In addition to ordinary shares, the articles of association may provide for one or more of the following types of shares:

(1) *Priority shares.* Priority shareholders have special rights by virtue of the articles of association. These rights may for instance relate to the appointment and dismissal of managing or supervisory directors or the amendment of the articles of association. There can be different classes of priority shares, usually specified in the articles of association as class A, B etc.

(2) *Preferred shares.* The holders of these shares have a preferred right to dividend and to the distributable proceeds in case of liquidation of the company. Common shareholders do not have pre-emptive rights with respect to the issue of preferred shares.

(3) *Depositary receipts.* Registered shares in a company are sometimes issued or transferred to an administration office (*administratiekantoor*), which is usually a foundation. The administration office in its turn issues depositary receipts of shares (*certificaten van aandelen*) which can be in registered or

in bearer form. The role of the administration office can be best compared to that of a 'trust' under English law.

The voting rights remain with the administration office and will be exercised by the administration office. All dividends received will be paid to the holders of the depositary receipts.

Depositary receipts may be convertible, partly convertible or non-convertible into shares.

All three types of shares are used in measures to minimise the power of the shareholders and—in the case of listed companies—to defend the company against hostile take-overs (see section **1.5.6**).

1.3.2   REGISTERED SHARES—TRANSFER—SHAREHOLDERS' REGISTER

Registered shares

The shares in a BV are always registered shares. The articles of association of an NV must provide whether the shares are in registered or in bearer form or that the shares can be issued in either form. If the articles of the NV provide that shares may be in either form, the NV must issue a bearer share in exchange for a registered share, and *vice versa*, at the shareholder's request, unless the articles of association provide otherwise. Registered shares do not (always) have to be fully paid-up when issued (see section **1.4.1**).

Transfer

Ownership of registered shares, in an NV or BV, can be transferred in two ways:
(1)   by private or notarial deed of transfer which is subsequently served upon the company by a bailiff (see **Introduction**); or
(2)   by a deed of transfer and written acknowledgement by the company after the deed has been submitted to it.

Acknowledgement by the company can be made by a person authorised to represent the company. To establish that the deed has actually been submitted to the company and as future evidence that the acknowledgement took place, it is practical to include the acknowledgement in the deed.

If the management of the company is opposed to the transfer, the manner of transfer as described in (1) will be more appropriate.

Proposed change in formalities

New legislation is pending which provides for more formalities in connection with the issue or transfer of registered shares. It is currently proposed that the deed of transfer should be a notarial deed.

Transfer of partly paid-up shares

If shares which have not yet been fully paid up, are transferred, acknowledgement of the transfer by the Company can only take place if the deed has a fixed date. A private (non-notarial) deed can be given a fixed date by registration of the deed in a register kept by the 'inspector of registration' (one of the tax inspectors). A notarial deed always has a fixed date.

Notwithstanding the transfer of shares which have not been fully paid up, each previous holder of such shares will remain liable, *vis-à-vis* the company, for payment of the outstanding amount.

The managing board (together with the supervisory board if there is one) may release a previous shareholder from this liability. However, the previous shareholder will remain liable for the outstanding amounts called within one year after the date of transfer.

Transfer in case of share certificates

If the company (this can only be an NV) has issued share certificates of registered shares, the requirements for transfer of registered shares are somewhat stricter. The articles of association may provide that the transfer by service of the deed upon the company can only validly take place if the share certificate is surrendered to the company at the same time. As proof of the transfer, the company will then make a note of the transfer on the share certificate or will issue a new certificate in the name of the new owner of the shares.

Acknowledgement of the deed of transfer of the registered shares is only valid if a note of the acknowledgement is made on the share certificate or if the share certificate is replaced by a new certificate in the name of the new shareholder.

Shareholders' register

The managing board of the company must keep a register of all holders of registered shares. The NV must only keep such a 'shareholders' register' if it has issued registered shares. The register contains the names and addresses of all holders of registered shares and the amount paid up on each share. The names and addresses of pledgees or holders of usufruct, together with any voting rights, are also recorded. At the request of a shareholder, a pledgee or a holder of usufruct the managing board must provide an extract from the shareholders' register which shows the specific right to the shares.

The shareholders' register must be kept at the working office of the company. Part of the register of an NV may be kept outside the Netherlands, if applicable legislation or stock exchange regulations abroad require this.

The information in the register on fully paid up shares is only available to shareholders and to pledgees or holders of usufruct who have voting rights. Information regarding shares which have not been fully paid up is available for public inspection. It should be emphasised that the entry in the shareholders' register is not a constitutive requirement for a valid issue, transfer, pledge etc of a share. Transfer of ownership of a share may have taken place without this having been recorded by the company. The register can therefore only serve as an indication of the persons holding the shares but never as conclusive evidence.

1.3.3   MANDATORY RESTRICTIONS ON TRANSFER OF REGISTERED SHARES

General

As stated above, the BV is required by law to provide in its articles of association for restriction on transfer of its shares. This is to ensure the 'private' nature of a BV.

The NV may restrict the transfer of its shares.

The BV can only restrict the transfer in two different manners described by statutory law (see further below). For the NV there are no specific statutory rules as to the manner of restricting transfer. For the BV as well as the NV restrictions may never be such as to render transferability of shares impossible or extremely difficult.

The Departmental Guidelines (see section **1.2.1** contain) further rules—for BV *and* NV—on how to restrict the transfer of shares. For the BV, these guidelines complement the statutory restriction provisions.

Unrestricted transfer to certain persons

The mandatory restrictions on transfer of shares in a BV do not have to apply to all transfers. Unless the articles of association provide otherwise, a shareholder of a BV may freely transfer one or more shares to his spouse, to a certain number of other blood relatives or relatives by marriage, to another shareholder of the company and to the company itself. The group of relatives may be further extended in the articles of association.

Types of restrictions

By statute, one of the two following types of restrictions must be provided for in the articles of association of a BV:

(1) a provision whereby all transfers of shares are subject to prior approval by a corporate body (including managing board and supervisory board);

(2) a provision whereby a shareholder who wishes to transfer shares must offer such shares to the other shareholders first.

A combination of the two types of restrictions is allowed. A different type of restriction for different shareholders or for different kinds of shares is also possible. Tighter restrictions than those provided for by law are allowed. For instance, the articles may impose certain conditions of quality on prospective shareholders, provided such conditions are not in violation of EC law. As referred to above, restrictions may not render a transfer impossible or extremely difficult.

(1) *Prior approval for share transfers.* The 'competent corporate body' is designated by the articles of association and may for instance be the managing board or the general meeting of shareholders. In the case of the NV, a third party may be designated to grant the approval.

The transfer must take place within three months after the approval. If the approval is refused, the competent corporate body must provide the transferor with the name(s) of one or more prospective parties who are willing to buy all the shares against payment in cash. If the competent corporate body fails to do so, the approval is deemed to have been granted.

The Departmental Guidelines provide that the articles of

association of the BV must set a certain period in which the competent corporate body must decide whether or not it will approve a proposed transfer. If no decision is taken, the transferor is free to transfer during three months after the end of the given period.

(2) *Offer to the other shareholders.* The articles of the BV may provide that the transferor must give the other shareholders a right of first refusal. According to the Departmental Guidelines it is possible to provide that the shares are first offered to certain (groups of) shareholders and that any remaining shares are subsequently offered to the other shareholders. No offer to a third party is permitted before all shareholders have received an offer. In the NV on the contrary, the articles of association may allow the offeror to offer the shares directly to third parties without offering the shares to the other shareholders first.

The restriction by right of first refusal may also include a provision that, if the other shareholders do not accept the offer, the transferor must offer the shares to other prospective buyers designated by a specified corporate body.

The offeror of shares in a BV is free in transferring his shares, during three months after it has been established that he cannot transfer all offered shares against payment in cash.

The articles of association of the BV may provide—and this may be useful to avoid lengthy offering procedures—that the shares do not have to be offered, if the transfer takes place with the written approval of the other shareholders.

Withdrawal of offer

In both systems of transfer restrictions (the prior approval system and the right of first refusal system), the transferor must have the right to withdraw his offer. He must, however, do this within one month after it has become known to him who the proposed buyers are and at what price he can sell.

Price of shares

With respect to the price of the offered shares, statutory law provides that both types of restrictions on transfer of shares in the BV must be such that the shareholder shall, if he so requests, receive a purchase price equal to the value of the shares as determined by one or more independent experts.

1.3.4 BEARER SHARES IN AN NV—TRANSFER

Bearer shares

Bearer shares (in an NV) may only be issued if this is provided for by the articles of association. The share is embodied in a certificate to bearer. As described in section **1.3.2**, registered shares may be exchanged for bearer shares and *vice versa*.

The company may not issue a bearer share unless the share has been paid up in full.

Transfer

Transfer of a bearer share is effected by delivery of the share certificate. In practice, however, most transfers of bearer shares—as these are mostly issued by listed companies—take place through the system of giro transfer (*giraal effectenverkeer*) (see further section **5.3.4**).

1.3.5 PLEDGE AND USUFRUCT OF SHARES

Procedure

The requirements for pledging registered shares or granting a right of usufruct (ie income or other proceeds) on registered shares are the same as for transfer (see section **1.3.2**) of registered shares. A deed of pledge or usufruct must be made and served upon the company or acknowledged by the company. If registered shares in an NV for which share certificates have been issued, are pledged or given in usufruct the acknowledgement of the deed is only valid if the interest is noted on the share certificates. A right of pledge on a bearer share is created by bringing the share certificate within the physical control of the pledgee or a third party appointed by the pledgor and pledgee. A right of usufruct with respect to a bearer share is created by delivery of the share certificate to the holder of the right of usufruct.

If the bearer shares have been admitted to the securities giro system, a right of pledge or usufruct can be established in accordance with special provisions of the Act on securities transactions by giro, by registration in the administration of the affiliated institution or the central depository (see section **5.3.4**).

Exclusion or restriction

The right to establish a usufruct on any shares and the right to pledge bearer shares may not be excluded or restricted by the articles of association. The right to pledge registered shares, however, can be restricted or excluded by the articles of association.

Right to vote

The right to vote will remain with the shareholder, unless it is provided upon the creation of the right of pledge or usufruct that the pledgee or holder of usufruct will have the right to vote on the share. If the pledgee or holder of usufruct is a person to whom the (registered!) shares cannot be freely transferred (ie if one of the restrictions on transfer as described in section **1.3.3** apply), he will not automatically have the right to vote:

(1)   if the prior approval of a corporate body is required for a transfer, the same corporate body must approve the granting (or transfer) of the voting rights to the pledgee or holder of the usufruct;

(2)   if the articles of association provide for a right of first refusal, the general meeting of shareholders must give such approval.

This prior approval is mandatory for a BV. In the articles of association of an NV other provisions may be made.

Other rights

The pledgee and the holder of usufruct are entitled to the dividend declared and usually have the same rights to attend general meetings of shareholders as holders of depositary receipts of shares (see section **1.3.1**) issued with the company's cooperation. The pledgee wishing to execute his right of pledge must comply with the transfer restrictions in the articles of association before disposing of or transferring the pledged shares. The disposal must be in accordance with mandatory provisions of Dutch law on pledge.

1.4   Capital

1.4.1   Minimum capital requirements

Definitions of capital

In Dutch company law a distinction is made between:

(1) Authorised capital (*maatschappelijk kapitaal*). This is the maximum amount as specified in the articles of association for which shares may be issued.

(2) Issued capital (*geplaatst kapitaal*). This is the total par value (see below) of the shares which have been issued by the company. When reference is made to '(share) capital', this usually means the issued capital.

(3) Paid-up capital (*gestort kapitaal*). This is the part of the issued share capital which has been paid up. The total amount paid for the shares may be higher than this paid-up capital if more than the par value of the shares was paid. The premium amount is called *agio* and is not a part of the 'paid-up capital'.

Minimum capital requirements

As a rule of mandatory law, the authorised, issued and paid-up capital of an NV must be Dfl 100,000.

In the case of a BV this minimum amount is (subject to future increases by royal decree) Dfl 40,000.

A further minimum requirement for the NV and the BV is that one fifth of the authorised share capital must be issued.

Bearer shares must always be fully paid up. Registered shares can be partly paid up with a minimum of 25 per cent of the par value of the shares.

Liability

The managing director(s) of a company will be personally liable for all acts of the company until the paid-up capital equals the higher of (i) the statutory minimum amount or (ii) an amount which equals 25 per cent of the issued capital.

As noted before, disadvantages of not fully paying up are that the shareholders of partly paid-up shares will remain liable to the company for the additional payment on the shares and that the transfer of partly paid-up shares is more complicated (see section **1.3.2**). The holders of partly paid-up shares must be registered in the trade register (see section **1.2.2**).

Par value

The authorised capital of a company and the par value of the shares are referred to in the articles of association and must be expressed in Dutch guilders. The par value of a share may be as low as Dfl 0.01. However, in practice most companies have shares in denominations of Dfl 100 or Dfl 1,000.

1.4.2 PAYMENT ON SHARES IN CASH

Procedure

Unless it is agreed that the shares are paid up in kind (see section **1.4.3**), payment is made in cash.

In case of payment in cash on shares before or at the incorporation of the company, one or more so-called 'bank statements' must be attached to the deed of incorporation. The bank statement must certify that the amounts which must be paid up on the shares to be issued at incorporation:

(1)   will be at the company's disposal immediately upon incorporation; or

(2)   were all placed at the same time—not earlier than five months before the date of incorporation—in a separate account which will be at the exclusive disposal of the company after the incorporation, provided that the company accepts these amounts in the deed of incorporation.

Withdrawal of cash

The amounts referred to in (2) may be withdrawn again and used for the company before its incorporation, ie for an NV io or a BV io (see section **1.2.4**). In order to avoid abuse of the 'b' bank statement, Dutch company law provides that the incorporators of the company will be liable *vis-à-vis* the company for compensation of those amounts withdrawn, until the company has explicitly ratified such withdrawals.

Payment in foreign currency

Payment in a foreign currency before or at incorporation is only allowed if the deed of incorporation permits it. Payment in a foreign currency on shares issued after incorporation requires the prior approval of the company. Payment on shares which are issued after incorporation is not subject to the requirement of a bank statement as referred to above. However, when payment on such shares is made in a foreign currency, a bank statement with respect to the exchange rate must be filed with the trade register within two weeks after payment is made.

1.4.3 CONTRIBUTION IN KIND—'QUASI' CONTRIBUTION

Contribution in kind

Contribution in kind on shares is possible provided the contribution can be valued by an economic standard. A right to the performance of labour or the rendering of services cannot be contributed.

The contribution must be made immediately upon—not necessarily at the same time as—the subscription to a share.

Approval by shareholders

As explained in section **1.2.4**, the company will only be bound by a contribution in kind made on its shares at the incorporation if a reference to such contribution is included in the deed of incorporation, ie approved by all incorporators. If the contribution in kind is made with respect to a later subscription to shares, the general meeting of shareholders or—if this authority is expressly delegated in the articles of association—the managing board must approve such contribution.

Description

If a contribution in kind is made—whether at the incorporation of the company or at a later issue of shares—a 'description' of the contribution must be made. The description states the value of the contribution and the valuation methods used. These valuation methods must be in accordance with generally accepted accounting standards. The description must refer to the condition of the contribution on a date which must be within five months before the incorporation or, as the case may be, within five months before the later issue of shares.

Accountant's statement

In addition to the description, Dutch law requires a statement from a chartered accountant that the value of the contribution to be made equals at least the amount to be paid up on the shares.

If the value of the contribution is known to have decreased substantially after the description is made, a second accountant's statement is required.

Exemption

Under certain strict conditions, a group company can be exempt from the obligation to make a description and to have an accountant's statement issued.

Further requirement

If contribution in kind is made at the incorporation, the incorporators are responsible for making the description. The accountant's statement—and in the case of an NV also the description itself—is attached to the deed of incorporation and will be available at the trade register for public inspection (see section **1.2.2**). The description of the contribution on shares in a BV is only available for inspection by shareholders and holders of depositary receipts.

If contribution in kind is made on shares issued after the incorporation of the company, the managing directors are responsible for making the description. Only the accountant's statement—in case of the BV and NV—must be filed with the trade register, within eight days after the subscription to the shares.

'Quasi' contribution

In order to avoid circumvention of the statutory requirements for contribution in kind to the detriment of creditors, a company is restricted in acquiring goods from its incorporators or shareholders. The restriction applies if:

(1)   the goods including receivables which are set off belonged to an incorporator or—in the case of a BV only—to a shareholder one year or less before the incorporation; and
(2)   the transaction to acquire such goods is entered into by the company during the two years following the first registration of the company with the trade register.

The approval of the general meeting of shareholders must be obtained for such a 'quasi' contribution. Moreover, the company must make a description and an accountant's statement must be issued, both similar to those required for a contibution in kind. If a transaction is entered into without the approval of the general meeting of shareholders or without an accountant's statement, the transaction may be declared null and void on behalf of the company.

Permitted transactions

Excluded from the restriction on 'quasi' contribution is any acquisition:

(1)   made at a public auction or at an exchange;
(2)   which, considering the terms of the transaction, is within the normal course of business of the company;
(3)   in respect of which an accountant's statement as required for a contribution in kind at incorporation is made; or
(4)   which results from a merger.

**1.4.4 PURCHASE BY THE COMPANY OF ITS SHARES—
FINANCIAL ASSISTANCE**

Subscription or re-purchase

The BV and the NV cannot subscribe to shares in their own capital but can, to a certain extent, purchase their own shares. A subsidiary cannot subscribe to shares in the capital of its parent company either; but a subsidiary may, by transfer, hold shares in the capital of its parent company in so far as the parent company itself may purchase shares in its own capital. 'Shares' include, in the context of the provisions regarding purchase by the company, depositary receipts of shares. The company may only purchase shares in its own capital which are fully paid up. A purchase of partly paid-up shares is void.

Re-purchase

The BV and the NV may in principle purchase (fully paid-up) shares in their own capital without limitation if no purchase price is due. Such purchase for no consideration (*om niet*) is valid under Dutch law. The company may also freely acquire shares by means of a universal succession of title (*onder algemene titel*). If the purchase of (fully paid-up) shares takes place against payment of a purchase price the company must meet the following conditions:

(1)   the purchase price may not exceed the amount of the distributable reserves (ie the company's net assets minus the paid-up and called capital and undistributable reserves);

(2)   the par value amount of shares in the company's capital held by the company and its subsidiaries may never exceed 10 per cent—in the case of an NV—and 50 per cent—in the case of a BV—of the issued capital of the company;

(3)   such purchase for consideration must be permitted by the articles of association; and

(4)   the general meeting of shareholders (or, in case of the BV, another corporate body) must have given authorisation to the managing board (or in case of the BV, another corporate body). The authorisation by the general meeting of an NV cannot be granted for a longer period than 18 months.

In case of purchase of shares for no consideration or by universal succession of title, the company may exceed the limitation of 10/50 per cent as referred to above under (2), but not for a longer period than three years.

Sanctions on violation

If the company purchases registered shares in its capital for consideration in violation of the requirements listed above, the purchase is void. Each managing director is liable for damages suffered by the seller acting in good faith. In case of bearer shares (in an NV) the shares purchased in violation of the rules will automatically be owned by the managing director(s), who will be liable for payment of the purchase price to the company.

Voting

The company or its subsidiaries may not vote on shares held by them in the capital of the company.

Financial assistance

The NV and—to a lesser extent—the BV are prohibited from inducing others to acquire shares in their capital by offering financial assistance.

The NV may not grant loans, provide security, guarantee a share price or otherwise guarantee or bind itself for the purpose of subscription to or acquisition by third parties of shares in its capital or in the capital of its subsidiary. The prohibition does not apply to the acquisition of listed shares by or for the account of employees of the NV.

For the BV the prohibition is the same, except that the BV may grant loans for the purpose of subscription to or acquisition of shares in its capital (this includes loans to employees for such purpose). However, the BV can only make such loans from its distributable reserves and in so far as the articles of association permit the making of these loans.

The statutory provisions do not provide for a sanction. It is generally believed that a transaction entered into in violation of these financial assistance provisions is null and void.

1.4.5 REDUCTION OF CAPITAL

Procedure

Reduction of the (issued) capital of a company can be realised by cancellation of shares or by reduction of the par value of the shares. Reduction may not result in the paid-up (and called) capital becoming less than the statutory minimum capital (see section **1.4.1**).

Cancellation of shares is possible with respect to:
(1) shares which are held by the company itself or depositary receipts of which are held by the company;
(2) shares of a certain class (for instance preferred shares) for which the articles of association provide that they can be cancelled upon redemption;
(3) shares which all shareholders agree to be cancelled on redemption.

The general meeting of shareholders must pass a resolution to reduce the capital by cancellation.

Cancellation of shares may be a solution for a company which has reached the 10/50 per cent threshold for purchasing shares in its own capital.

The second type of reduction, ie reduction of the par value of the shares, can only be effected by an amendment of the articles of association.

A reduction of the par value of the shares is allowed without redemption and without a release of the obligation to pay up, provided, however, that reduction takes place *pro rata* to all shares of the same class. This *pro rata* requirement may be waived.

Protection of creditors

Additional provisions exist to protect the creditors of a company which has decided to reduce its capital. The shareholders' resolution to reduce the capital must be filed with the trade register and announced in a national daily newspaper.

If so requested, the company must—with some exceptions—give security for (or guarantee) the payment of a claim of a creditor of the company.

A creditor can oppose the resolution to reduce the capital by starting proceedings before the District Court within two months after the announcement of the resolution. The creditor must state in the proceedings the security or guarantee required by him.

The resolution to reduce the capital will not take effect until the period of two months, during which opposition can be filed, has ended. If opposition proceedings have been instituted, these will further delay the effectuation of the resolution to reduce the capital.

1.4.6 INCREASE OF CAPITAL—ISSUE OF RIGHTS TO ACQUIRE SHARES—PRE-EMPTIVE RIGHTS

Issue of shares

The capital of the company can be increased by a new issue of shares provided that the authorised capital permits a new issue (see section **1.4.1**). If not, the articles of association must be amended to increase the authorised capital.

The issue of new shares by the NV is subject to more extensive requirements than an issue by the BV. In the NV and the BV the general meeting of shareholders has the authority to decide on the issue of new shares. This authority may be delegated to another corporate body, for instance the managing board. Such delegation may take place by the general meeting of shareholders or may be provided for in the articles of association. In the NV, the delegation can never be for a longer period than five years. The delegation cannot be withdrawn unless this is provided in the resolution to delegate. The delegation can be renewed each time for a maximum of five years. A resolution to delegate must be filed with the trade register.

In the BV the delegation does not have to be limited to a certain period. The general meeting of shareholders in the BV may at any time withdraw a delegation whether or not the delegation has been limited to a certain period.

Additional requirements for NVs

For the NV additional requirements apply. If there are different classes of shares, each group of shareholders whose rights are prejudiced by the issue of new shares will have to approve the issue in addition to the resolution by the general meeting of shareholders. The NV must furthermore file, with the trade register, the resolution to issue new shares and to delegate its authority. This filing must be made within eight days after the resolution was passed. The NV must also register details of each actual issue of shares.

Issue of rights to shares

All requirements described above likewise apply to the issue of rights to acquire shares, such as convertible bonds, options or warrants. When those rights are exercised, the requirements do not have to be complied with again. A new resolution does not have to be passed nor does the conversion from the said rights into shares have to be registered. (It should be noted, however, that the company must annually inform the trade register of its issued share capital.)

Pre-emptive rights

In the NV and the BV existing shareholders have a statutory pre-emptive right to newly issued shares in proportion to the par value of their shareholdings. Holders of shares which are not common shares do not have such pre-emptive rights. Shareholders do not have a pre-emptive right:

(1)   to shares issued to employees of the company or of a group company;

(2)   to shares in an NV which are issued against contribution in kind (unless the articles of association of the NV provide otherwise), for instance if shares are issued against contribution of (part of) an enterprise;

(3)   if their pre-emptive rights are excluded or limited by the articles of association—this is only possible in a BV—or by a resolution of the general meeting of shareholders (or the corporate body delegated to decide on the issue of new shares);

(4)   to shares which are not common shares.

The statutory pre-emptive rights should be distinguished from pre-emptive rights based on the articles of association to which the abovementioned provisions do not apply.

Pre-emption in respect of rights to shares

When rights to acquire shares are granted by a company, the shareholders have the same statutory pre-emptive rights. No statutory pre-emptive rights exist with respect to shares issued to a person who exercises a previously obtained right to acquire shares.

1.5   GENERAL MEETING OF SHAREHOLDERS— SHAREHOLDERS' RIGHTS

1.5.1   INTRODUCTION

The shareholders of a Dutch company are collectively referred to as the general meeting of shareholders (*algemene vergadering van aandeelhouders*). Book 2 of the Civil Code provides that the general meeting of shareholders has the authority which has not been conferred upon the managing board or on other corporate bodies. This authority widely varies depending on the extent to which the powers of the general meeting have been delegated by the articles of association. However, pursuant to mandatory provisions of Dutch company law the general meeting always retains final authority with respect to:

(1) the amendment of the articles of association;
(2) the liquidation of the company;
(3) the adoption of the annual accounts of the company (however, see section **1.7.3**);
(4) the appointment and dismissal of the managing directors of the company and of two thirds of the supervisory directors (however, see section **1.7.3**);
(5) the issue of shares, the reduction of capital and the purchase by the company of shares in its own capital.

This authority may be limited by the articles of association but can never be entirely taken away.

By 'oligarchic' measures, the power of the common shareholders of the company can be greatly diminished (see section **1.5.6**).

1.5.2   CONVENING THE MEETINGS OF SHAREHOLDERS—LOCATION—SHAREHOLDERS' RESOLUTIONS

Annual and other meetings

No distinction between different types of meetings of shareholders is made. It is merely provided by statute that a meeting of shareholders must be held at least once a year. This annual meeting must be held within six months after the end of the company's financial year. A shorter period may be provided by the articles of association. At this meeting the annual accounts of the company are adopted (approved in a 'large' company).

In addition to the annual meeting, other meetings of shareholders can be held during the year. In the NV a meeting of shareholders must be held if the company suffers losses resulting in the company's equity falling below an amount equal to half of the paid-up and called part of the company's capital.

If there are different classes of shares, the holders of a certain class (for instance the priority) will have their own meetings in addition to the general meetings.

Authority to call meetings

The meetings of shareholders may be called by the managing board and by the supervisory board. Other persons may be designated in the articles of association to call the meetings, for instance individual managing directors or even shareholders.

Shareholders and/or holders of depositary receipts issued with the company's cooperation who jointly represent 10 per cent of the issued capital, may under certain circumstances seek authorisation from the president of the District Court to call a meeting of shareholders.

If the persons responsible for calling meetings of shareholders fail to call the meetings required by law or by the articles of association, each individual shareholder or holder of depositary receipts may be authorised by the president of the District Court to call such meeting himself.

Notice convening the meetings

The shareholders and the holders of depositary receipts issued with the company's cooperation are called to attend the meetings of shareholders. In the NV, notice convening the meeting is usually given by publication in a national daily newspaper. In the BV, notice to the shareholders is given by mail and to the holders of depositary receipts by a notice in a national daily newspaper (unless the articles provide otherwise). The notices must contain or in certain cases refer to the agenda of the meeting. The meeting must be convened no later than 15 days before the date of the meeting. If these statutory requirements for the convening of meetings of shareholders are not adhered to, the general meeting of shareholders may nevertheless pass a valid resolution if the entire issued capital is represented and the resolution is passed by a unanimous vote.

Location of the meetings

As a general rule, the meetings of shareholders are held in the Netherlands at the place stated in the articles of association, or otherwise at the company's principal place of business. The meetings may be held outside the Netherlands but in such

meeting valid resolutions can only be passed if all shareholders
are represented.

Shareholders' resolutions

The articles of association of a company may—and often
do—provide that a resolution by the general meeting of
shareholders may be passed outside the actual meeting, unless
depositary receipts with the company's cooperation or bearer
shares have been issued. Such resolution is only valid if passed by
unanimous vote and if the votes have been cast in writing (which
can be by telecopier, telex, etc).

1.5.3   RIGHTS OF THE SHAREHOLDERS AT THE MEETING— VOTING RIGHTS—SHAREHOLDERS' AGREEMENTS

Rights at the meeting

Each shareholder has the right to attend the general meeting,
to address the meeting and to exercise his voting rights. He can be
represented by another person holding a written proxy but this
right of representation may be limited by the articles of
association. The same applies to the holders of depositary
receipts issued with the company's cooperation except that these
holders do not have voting rights (see section **1.3.1**). The
managing directors and supervisory directors also attend the
general meetings and have an advisory role. They must provide
the general meeting with all information it requests, unless this is
against vital interests of the company.

Voting rights

Each shareholder—in this context including holders of
usufruct or pledge having voting rights—has at least one vote.
Dutch law does not permit the issue of non-voting shares. If all
shares have the same par value, each shareholder has as many
votes as shares. If the shares of the company have different par
values, the number of votes of each shareholder is determined by
dividing the total par value of his shares by the par value of the
smallest share issued by the company. The number of votes to be
cast by one shareholder may be limited by the articles of
association. No votes can be cast on shares which belong to the
company itself or to its subsidiary.

Resolutions are passed by an absolute majority of the votes

cast, unless statutory law or the articles of association require a greater majority, a special majority or even a unanimous vote. In a few cases, a quorum is required by statutory law. For instance a resolution by the NV's general meeting of shareholders to reduce its capital must be passed with a two-thirds' majority if less than half of the issued share capital is represented at the meeting. A quorum in the sense that the entire issued capital must be represented at the meeting is sometimes required, for instance when a resolution is passed in a general meeting, which was not convened in accordance with the statutory rules. A quorum may also be provided for in the articles of association.

Shareholders' agreements

The articles of association of a Dutch company cannot provide for the manner in which shareholders exercise their voting rights.

On the other hand, agreements between shareholders which provide how the shareholders will vote are, as a general rule, valid agreements under Dutch law. They may not, however, violate public interest and good morals.

For instance, an agreement resulting in a shareholders' resolution which violates mandatory statutory law or the articles of association is considered to be against public interest and is therefore invalid. Furthermore, an agreement which forces a shareholder to vote, at unspecified future occasions, in a certain way or at another person's instructions may be held invalid by a Dutch court.

It should be noted that a vote exercised by a shareholder in violation of a valid shareholders' agreement but in accordance with the articles of association, will be a valid vote. Such shareholder can only be sued for breach of contract.

1.5.4 ANNULMENT AND NULLITY OF RESOLUTIONS

General

A resolution of the general meeting or of another corporate body such as the managing or supervisory board can be null and void by operation of law or can be annulled by the District Court. The provisions in Book 2 Civil Code on this subject were slightly changed on 1 January 1992. The new provisions are summarised in this paragraph.

Nullity

A resolution is null and void if it breaches (mandatory) statutory law or the articles of association. Examples of such void resolutions are:

(1)   a resolution of the general meeting to issue shares in excess of the authorised capital;

(2)   a resolution of the managing board to appoint supervisory directors;

(3)   a resolution of the general meeting to amend the articles of association without the prior approval of the supervisory board if that is required by the articles of association.

A null and void resolution may—in certain circumstances—be ratified.

Annulment

For annulment of a resolution a decision by the District Court is required. Proceedings for annulment can—depending on the circumstances—be instituted by an interested party having a reasonable interest or by the company itself.

Grounds for annulment are:

(1)   breach of the statutory provisions or provisions in the articles of association, which provide for the manner in which resolutions are passed (except for the provisions which require a prior act of or notice to another corporate body, see example (3) above).

For example: provisions which provide for the convening of general meetings or require a certain majority or quorum in those meetings;

(2)   breach of 'reasonableness and fairness'.

It is a rule of company law that the company and its corporate bodies must act *vis-à-vis* each other in accordance with 'reasonableness and fairness';

(3)   breach of 'regulations' (*reglement*).

For instance: regulations on decision making by the managing board (see section **1.6.1**).

A resolution as referred to in (1) can—in certain circumstances—be 'confirmed'.

Third parties

The nullity or the annulment of a resolution cannot be invoked against a third party acting in good faith. A null or annulled appointment of a managing or supervisory director may, however, be invoked against the appointed director.

Other rules

Nullity or annulment may also be based on other provisions of statutory law. For example, on the Works Council Act (see section **1.11.4**) or on the statutory provisions regarding inquiry (see section **1.9.3**).

1.5.5 ALLOCATION OF PROFITS—DIVIDEND

Unless the articles of association provide otherwise, the shareholders of the company are entitled to the profits. The articles of association of the company usually state that the profits are 'at the disposal' of the general meeting of shareholders, ie that the general meeting decides on the actual allocation of the profits. Dividend can be paid to the shareholders only to the extent that the company's equity exceeds the sum of the amount of the paid-up and called part of the capital plus the mandatory reserves.

All shareholders will share equally in the profits of the company in proportion to the amount of their shares, unless the articles of association provide otherwise. Preferred shares (see section **1.3.1**) are an example of a deviation from the equality between shareholders.

The payment of dividend is made after the adoption (or approval) of the annual accounts from which it emerges that such payment is permitted.

Interim dividends can be paid provided the articles of association permit this and only to the extent that there are distributable reserves (see above).

Dividend may be paid in cash or in the form of shares or rights to shares (claims or warrants).

1.5.6 PROTECTIVE AND OLIGARCHIC MEASURES

Types of measures

In section **1.3.1** depositary receipts of shares, priority shares and preferred shares were briefly discussed.

In listed NVs the following protective measures are regularly used to avoid a hostile take-over:

(1) The articles of association provide that the shares in the

company are held by an administration office which issues in exchange depositary receipts of shares. The administration office retains the voting rights.

(2) The company issues preferred shares—the articles must allow such issue—to a 'friendly' third party, usually a foundation; the company thus creates more 'friendly' votes at the general meeting of shareholders.

(3) Priority shares, conferring special rights to the holder, are issued by the company to a third party, again usually a foundation.

In BVs and unlisted NVs measure 1 or measure 3 is also often used, but as an oligarchic measure rather than as a protective measure.

Rules of the Amsterdam Stock Exchange

In 1989 the Amsterdam Stock Exchange imposed new restrictive rules regarding the use by listed companies of protective measures. The restrictions are included in the Rules relating to the requirements for listing of the Amsterdam Stock Exchange, as attachment X (see section **5.3.2**). Under these new rules, the issue of depositary receipts which cannot be cancelled, is not allowed. Furthermore, the administration office which holds the shares and issues the depositary receipts, must be independent.

The issue of preferred shares to a 'friendly' third party is also subject to the requirement that such third party is independently managed. Independent in the context of these two defensive actions means that managing or supervisory directors of the company or other persons connected to the company may not have a majority in the board of the foundation, which is usually created for the purpose of such actions.

The Stock Exchange is less strict on the issue of priority shares. *Managing* directors of the company may not hold more than 50 per cent of the priority shares or more than 50 per cent of the voting rights in the board of the legal entity holding the priority shares. Other persons connected to the company are not restricted in the same way.

If, for instance, the priority shares would be held by a foundation, the board of this foundation may consist of 50 per cent managing directors and 50 per cent supervisory directors (or of 100 per cent supervisory directors).

In attachment X the number of defensive actions which may be used simultaneously is limited by the Stock Exchange to two actions at the same time.

1.5.7 DISCLOSURE OF MAJOR HOLDINGS IN LISTED COMPANIES

Present regulations

At present there is no statutory obligation to disclose major shareholdings in Dutch companies. There is only an obligation on a company listed on the Amsterdam Stock Exchange to inform the Stock Exchange Association when a shareholder acquires 20 per cent or more of the issued capital, provided the company is aware of this (see also section **5.3.2**).

Pending legislation

In compliance with the EC Directive of 12 December 1988 (Official Journal 1989, L348/62) regarding the disclosure of major holdings in listed companies, a new Act on such disclosure is pending in parliament. The Act came into force in February 1992. Under the proposed Act a shareholder of a Dutch listed company must immediately notify the company and the Minister of Finance if the number of shares held by him or votes exercisable by him exceeds or falls below a certain threshold.

The Minister of Finance has delegated his powers under the Act to the Securities Board (see section **5.1.3**).

In determining the percentage held, the shareholder must, *inter alia*, include depositary receipts of shares and rights to acquire shares as well as shares or voting rights held by its subsidiaries. The Act does not apply to members of stock exchanges within the EC and intermediaries who are allowed to act as such.

Various thresholds for disclosure apply: 5 per cent, 10 per cent, 25 per cent, 50 per cent and 66 $\frac{2}{3}$ per cent of the issued capital or the exercisable votes.

The company must immediately publish the contents of the disclosure in each country in which the shares are officially listed. The Minister of Finance, or, in some cases, the Securities Board, may exempt the company from this obligation.

A shareholder who holds more than 5 per cent of the shares or votes on the day the Act comes into force must notify the company and the Securities Board within 30 days thereafter.

Violation of the Act is an economic offence under the Act on economic offences. In addition, the Act provides for rather extreme civil sanctions to be imposed by the District Courts upon application by certain parties. These sanctions include:

(1) suspension or annulment of resolutions of the general meeting of shareholders;

(2) suspension of the non-disclosing shareholder's voting rights;

(3) a prohibition against this shareholder to acquire shares or other rights in the company.

1.6 MANAGEMENT OF THE COMPANY AND SUPERVISION OF MANAGEMENT

1.6.1 DUTIES AND AUTHORITY OF THE MANAGING BOARD

General

The managing board (*het bestuur* or *de directie*) is charged with the management of the company. The management is autonomous within the limits of the law and the articles of association. It does not have to take instructions from any other corporate body unless specifically provided otherwise in the articles of association. The Departmental Guidelines limit this possibility. This was explicitly stated by the Supreme Court in its *Forum Bank* decision 1955.

Restrictions of authority

The power of the managing board can be—and often is—restricted in the articles of association by providing that certain important decisions are subject to the prior approval of the general meeting of shareholders or the supervisory board. Prior approval may also be required from the collective holders of priority shares.

These restrictions on the managing board's authority do not have external effect. The company may not invoke the absence of required approval against third parties.

In the case of a 'large' company, prior approval by the supervisory board of certain management decisions is provided for by law (see section **1.7.3**).

Decision-making

There are no specific statutory rules regarding the decision-making by the managing board. Valid decisions by the managing board do not require that a meeting is held at which all managing directors are present. However, as a general rule, all managing directors must have been given the opportunity to attend the meeting in which a decision was made. The articles of association may contain provisions, for instance regarding a quorum or a certain majority of votes in board meetings. Sometimes the managing board is authorised by the articles of association to make its own regulations (*reglement*).

Resolutions of the managing board may, under certain circumstances, be null and void or be annulled (see section **1.5.4**).

1.6.2 APPOINTMENT AND DISMISSAL OF MANAGING DIRECTORS

Composition

The managing board consists of one or more managing directors (*bestuurders* or *directeuren*). Legal entities may also be managing directors. Further quality requirements may be imposed on the managing directors by the articles of association, provided they do not make the appointment of directors too difficult. Nationality requirements may not violate EC law. Appointment, dismissal or suspension of managing directors must be registered with the trade register. Third parties may rely on the information as filed with the trade register (see section **1.2.2**).

Appointment

The first directors of the company are appointed in the deed of incorporation (see section **1.2.4**). After incorporation, the managing directors are appointed by the general meeting of shareholders, unless the company is a 'large' NV or BV (see section **1.7.3**). The general meeting will decide by an absolute majority. The articles of association may provide for a greater majority or may require a certain quorum.

Binding nominations

The authority of the general meeting of shareholders to appoint managing directors can be considerably reduced by granting another person or corporate body the right to make a 'binding nomination'. Two persons for each vacancy must be named. The right to make the binding nomination can be granted to the supervisory board, if there is one, or for instance to the holders of priority shares, the managing board itself or even an outsider. The law prescribes that the general meeting shall always have the possibility to resolve that a nomination made is not binding, provided such resolution is passed by a two-thirds' majority of the votes cast at a meeting at which more than 50 per cent of the issued capital is represented. The articles of association may provide for less stringent requirements to set aside binding nominations. These requirements may not be made more restrictive.

In a 'large' NV or BV the possibility of binding nominations does not exist.

Suspension and dismissal

The managing directors are dismissed or suspended by the general meeting of shareholders. The articles of association may provide for a special majority in the general meeting but this majority may never be greater than a two-thirds majority representing at least one half of the issued capital.

If there is a supervisory board in the company, it may also suspend managing directors unless the articles of association provide otherwise. The general meeting of shareholders may at all times set aside this suspension by the supervisory board.

The rules regarding suspension and dismissal are different in 'large' NVs and BVs (see section **1.7.3**).

Provisional management

Dismissal of a managing director must not result in the company being left without any management. The articles of association must therefore always contain provisions regarding the manner in which the company is provisionally managed when managing directors are absent or prevented from acting, for instance in case of dismissal. If the company has a supervisory board, the articles often provide that a supervisory director will provisionally manage the company.

Employment law

A managing director is usually also an 'employee' of the

company. This means that if he is dismissed, he may also seek protection in employment law. However, the position of a managing director is in certain respects different from that of other employees. For instance, for the termination of an employment agreement with a managing director a dismissal licence by the Regional Director for Employment Policy is not required. (See further section **2.7** on termination of employment agreements.)

1.6.3   PERSONAL LIABILITY OF MANAGING DIRECTORS

Special liability

As mentioned in section **1.2.2** and section **1.4.1**, each managing director is personally liable for all acts of the company before the company is filed for registration or before the minimum requirements for the paid-up capital of the company have been fulfilled.

Liability to the company

As a general rule, each managing director must properly perform the duties assigned to him and is personally liable *vis-à-vis* the company if he fails to do so. If a matter is within the responsibility of two or more managing directors, each is jointly and severally liable unless he proves that he cannot be blamed for the shortcoming and has not been negligent in preventing the consequences of such shortcoming. The managing director(s) whose duties did not include the given matter may be excluded from liability. However, no managing director can be excluded from responsibility for the general management of the company. The managing director who has not properly performed his duties can only be sued by the company itself, not by, for instance, a creditor.

External liability in bankruptcy

Since 1987, there are special provisions regarding personal liability of managing directors in case of bankruptcy of the company. If the management of the company has improperly performed its duties and if it may be assumed that this is an important cause of the bankruptcy, each managing director is personally liable for such debts of the company as remain unpaid upon liquidation of the company. Any person who (co-)determined the policy of the company as if he were a managing director is also liable.

If the management has failed to keep its books properly or has failed to publish its annual accounts in accordance with the statutory provisions, mismanagement is presumed to have occurred and to have been an important cause of the bankruptcy.

A managing director who can prove that he cannot be blamed for the mismanagement, cannot be held liable.

Other external liability

In addition to this personal liability in case of the company's bankruptcy, the managing directors are also personally liable to any third party for damages suffered as a result from a misrepresentation in the annual accounts, annual report or interim statements of the company provided these were published.

Liability of legal entity

A legal entity may be liable as managing director of the company. In that case each person who was a managing director of that legal entity at the time the liability arose is also personally liable. Such person cannot 'hide' behind the legal entity which formally manages the company.

1.6.4 AUTHORITY TO REPRESENT THE COMPANY—*ULTRA VIRES*

Power to bind the company

The managing board as a whole and each managing director separately are authorised to represent the company, at law and otherwise. Alternatively, the articles of association may provide that:

(1) in addition to the managing board itself, only one or more managing directors may represent the company;

(2) a managing director may only act jointly with one or more managing directors or other persons; or

(3) other persons, for instance so-called *procuratiehouders* (holders of a proxy), have authority to represent the company.

Only these restrictions on the authority of the managing directors to bind the company can be invoked by the company against third parties. The company must, however, have registered these restrictions with the trade register. If it has not done so, the restrictions cannot be invoked against the other party who was unaware of the restrictions.

Restrictions without 'external effect'

The articles may further restrict the authority to represent the company. For instance certain acts of managing directors may be made subject to prior approval by the supervisory board or by the general meeting of shareholders. Such further restrictions, however, may not be invoked by or against third parties.

Ultra vires

A transaction entered into by a person who was authorised to represent the company can nevertheless be annulled in case of *ultra vires*. The slightly revised art 7 of Book 2 Civil Code, which came into force on 1 January 1992, provides that a legal act executed by the company can be annulled if the objects of the company were transgressed and the other party knew or should have known this without having investigated this himself. Only the company (or the receiver in the company's bankruptcy), *not* the other party to the transaction, can invoke this ground for annulment.

The objects of the company are often described in very broad terms. It is, however, possible that a transaction which falls within the defined objects of the company but violates the vital interests of the company, may be *ultra vires*. This might be the case when a company gives an unlimited security for the obligations of its parent company in connection with a transaction from which it does not benefit itself.

Statute of limitations

After three years, the company can no longer take action to have *ultra vires* transactions annulled. After this period, it may only raise the *ultra vires* argument as a defence in proceedings brought against it.

Ratification

The possibility of annulment may create an uncertain situation for the other party. In order to end this uncertainty, the other party may set a reasonable period during which the company must choose either to confirm the transaction or to have it annulled. If the company does not act during such period it cannot have the transaction annulled afterwards.

1.6.5 DUTIES OF SUPERVISORY BOARD

General

The articles of association of a 'normal' NV or BV may provide for a supervisory board (*raad van commissarissen*). In a 'large' NV or BV, the establishment of a supervisory board is mandatory (see further section **1.7.1** on the supervisory board in 'large' companies).

A supervisory board may be established for various reasons:
(1)   in general, the presence of a second 'tier' in the management of the company may serve the purpose of 'checks and balances';
(2)   the supervisory board may be useful to involve independent experts in the decision making process within the company;
(3)   in family business or joint ventures certain family or joint venture representatives may wish to exercise influence in addition to their powers in the shareholders' meetings;
(4)   the Dutch government or one or more banks may require a supervisory board in which they can be represented.

Duties

The supervisory board's duties are to supervise the managing board's policy and the general course of business in the company and to render advice to the managing board. If there is a supervisory board, the articles of association usually provide that the managing board must obtain the supervisory board's consent for certain management decisions (NB: the absence of such consent may not be invoked by or against third parties).

In the performance of its duties, the supervisory board shall at all times be guided by the interests of the company.

All information which the supervisory board may require for the proper performance of its duties must be supplied to it by the managing board.

In addition to its general duties of supervision and advice, the supervisory board has some specific duties:
(1)   the articles of association often provide that the supervisory board or a supervisory director will provisionally manage

the company if the managing directors are absent or prevented from acting;

(2) if there is a conflict of interest between the company and one or more managing directors, the company will be represented by supervisory directors unless the articles of association provide otherwise (NB: the general meeting of shareholders may at all times appoint one or more other representatives);

(3) the supervisory board may suspend managing directors (unless the articles of association provide otherwise);

(4) the supervisory board may convene a general meeting of shareholders;

(5) the supervisory directors sign the annual accounts together with the managing directors and the supervisory board may instruct the auditing of the annual accounts if the general meeting fails to do this (see section **1.10.2**);

(6) at least one of the supervisory directors must be present at the meetings which the management holds with the works council of the company (if there is one) (see section **1.11.3**).

The articles of association may give further tasks to the supervisory board.

1.6.6 APPOINTMENT AND DISMISSAL OF SUPERVISORY DIRECTORS—LIABILITY OF SUPERVISORY DIRECTORS

Composition and appointment

The supervisory board consists of one or more natural persons. The supervisory directors cannot be older than 72 years. Quality requirements may be made subject to the same limitations as apply with respect to managing directors (see section **1.6.2**). Supervisory directors are appointed by the general meeting of shareholders, with the exception of those which have been appointed by the deed of incorporation. The provisions for appointment (and dismissal) of supervisory directors in a 'large' company are different (see section **1.7.2**).

The articles of association may provide that one third of the supervisory board is appointed by another party than the general meeting of shareholders, for instance by the holders of bonds issued by the company, by a government agency or a trade union.

The articles of association may also allow a 'binding

nomination' to be made by another corporate body or person subject to the same rules as apply in the case of managing directors (see section **1.6.2**).

Suspension and dismissal

Supervisory directors are dismissed or suspended by the same persons or entity who or which can appoint them.

Liability

If a supervisory director performs acts of management pursuant to a provision in the articles of association or a resolution of the shareholders he shall be deemed to have acted as managing director and shall be liable as a managing director (see section **1.6.3**). This may occur for instance if the managing directors are prevented from acting or if there is a conflict of interest between the managing directors and the company.

In the performance of his duties as supervisory director (this includes approving the acts of the managing board!) the supervisory director can also be held liable, both by the company itself or by third parties. Most provisions regarding the liability of managing directors likewise apply to supervisory directors, but only to the extent that the supervisory director did not fulfil his specific supervisory duties (see further section **1.6.3**).

1.7 LARGE NVS AND BVS

1.7.1 CRITERIA—TRANSITION PERIOD

General

When a company is a 'large' company, it will become subject to the so-called 'structure regime'. Under this regime a company must have a supervisory board. This supervisory board will be appointed according to a different procedure (see section **1.7.2**) and will have more extensive powers than a supervisory board in a 'normal' company (see section **1.7.3**).

NB: To the extent that they are not contrary to the 'structure' provisions, all other provisions of Book 2 Civil Code will apply likewise to 'large' companies.

Criteria

A company is subject to the structure regime if:

(1) the sum of its issued capital and its reserves is at least Dfl22.5m according to its balance sheet;

(2) the company or a dependent company has established a works council pursuant to a legal obligation; and

(3) the company and its dependent companies together normally employ at least 100 employees in the Netherlands.

It follows that the number of employees and the existence of a works council in its 'dependent' companies are relevant in determining whether a company is subject to the structure regime.

A company is a 'dependent' company if:

(1) more than 50 per cent of its issued capital is held by the (large) company concerned or one or more dependent companies, alone or jointly; or

(2) if the company is a partnership, its business is registered in the trade register and the (large) company concerned or a dependent company is fully liable as a partner for its debts.

Transition period

If a company meets the criteria of a 'large' company, it will not immediately become subject to the structure regime. At first, it will only have to file a statement with the trade register that it complies with the criteria. The statement must be filed within two months after the adoption or approval of the annual accounts. The statement can be cancelled if the company no longer meets the criteria. When the statement has been registered for three consecutive years, the company will become subject to the structure regime. It must by that time have conformed its articles of association to the structure provisions.

1.7.2 COMPOSITION OF THE SUPERVISORY BOARD— APPOINTMENT—DISMISSAL

Composition

The supervisory board in a large company must have three members. Excluded from membership are:

(1) employees of the company or of a 'dependent' company;

(2) officers or employees of a trade union which is involved in the company.

In addition, the supervisory directors in Dutch companies

must be natural persons and may not be older than 72 years (see section **1.6.6**).

Appointment

In respect of the appointment of supervisory directors, a system of so-called 'controlled cooptation' applies. There are two important aspects to this system:

(1) the supervisory board appoints its own members (cooptation);

(2) the general meeting—or a delegated 'committee of shareholders'—and the works council of the company—or of a dependent company—can make a non-binding recommendation for a new member and have a qualified veto right (codetermination).

The supervisory board must inform the general meeting, the works council and the managing board which person it proposes to appoint. The supervisory board may always ignore the recommendations made. The general meeting and the works council can, however, object against the proposed appointment on a limited number of grounds. The most important ground of objection is that as a result of the proposed appointment the supervisory board will not be 'suitably composed'.

If the parties cannot agree, the proposed appointment may nevertheless be made if—on the application of the supervisory board—the Enterprise Division of the Court of Appeal in Amsterdam (see **Introduction**) has declared the objection unfounded.

Appointment by general meeting and by the government

If there are no supervisory directors (yet), the general meeting of shareholders will appoint them. The articles of association may give authority to the government—local or central—to appoint one or more supervisory directors.

A right to make recommendations and a qualified veto right will apply in respect of such appointment by the general meeting or the government.

Term of office and dismissal

The supervisory directors in a large company must resign no later than four years after their appointment. Re-appointment is common.

A supervisory director can only be dismissed by the Enterprise Division of the Court of Appeal in Amsterdam on certain grounds. The supervisory board itself can suspend a supervisory director; but the suspension is terminated automatically if an application to the Enterprise Division for the dismissal of this director has not been made within one month following suspension.

1.7.3 POWERS OF THE SUPERVISORY BOARD UNDER THE STRUCTURE REGIME

Appointment and dismissal of managing directors

The managing directors of a 'large' company are always appointed by the supervisory board. This power may not be limited by any system of binding nominations. The supervisory board must only 'inform' the general meeting of the proposed appointment.

The supervisory board also has the exclusive right to dismiss and suspend managing directors. In case of dismissal, it must, however, 'consult' the general meeting first.

NB: The works council in the 'large' company has a statutory right to render advice on the appointment and dismissal of managing directors (see section **1.11.4**).

Adoption of annual accounts

The supervisory board adopts the annual accounts. It subsequently submits the accounts to the general meeting for its approval and at the same time to the works council for discussion.

The general meeting cannot amend the accounts, it can only give or withhold its approval.

Approval of certain management decisions

In a 'normal' company, a right of approval of certain management decisions can be granted to the supervisory board by the articles of association.

Under the structure regime a number of decisions by the managing board are by statute subject to approval by the supervisory board:

(1) the issue or acquisition by the company of shares in the company or the issue by the company of debt instruments;

(2) cooperation in the issue of depositary receipts for shares in the company;

(3) an application for or withdrawal of listing of the securities referred to in (1) or (2);

(4) the company or a 'dependent' company entering into or terminating a continuing cooperation with another company;

(5) the company or its 'dependent' company acquiring shares in the capital of another company the value of which equals at least a quarter of the issued capital and reserves of the acquiring company, or a considerable increase or decrease of such participation;

(6) making an investment which requires at least one quarter of the issued capital and reserves of the company;

(7) a proposal to amend the articles of association;

(8) a proposal to wind up the company;

(9) an application for bankruptcy (*faillissement*) or for a moratorium of payment (*surséance van betaling*);

(10) the termination of the employment of a considerable number of employees of the company or of a 'dependent' company, within a short period;

(11) a drastic change in the working conditions of a considerable number of such employees;

(12) a proposal to reduce the issued capital.

The absence of the supervisory board's approval cannot be invoked against third parties. (See section **1.5.4** about the internal effect of non-compliance.) By articles of association the list of decisions referred to above can be extended further.

1.7.4 MITIGATED REGIME—COMPLETE EXEMPTION—DISPENSATION

Mitigated regime

A 'large' company which is part of an international concern or joint venture with more than 50 per cent of its employees outside the Netherlands may, by statute, only be partly subject to the structure regime. Under this 'mitigated regime' the supervisory board does not have the right to approve the annual accounts and to appoint and dismiss managing directors. As in a 'normal' company, these powers are vested with the general meeting of shareholders.

NB: The company must file the statement as referred to in section **1.7.1** and must have complied with the mitigated regime after three years.

Exemption

A 'large' company can be completely exempted from the provisions of the structure regime. The cases in which the company is exempt can be summarised as follows:

(1) the company is a 'dependent' company of a legal entity which is itself subject to the structure regime or the mitigated regime;

(2) the company is only a 'holding' company in an international concern;

(3) the company is only acting as a service company within an international concern; or

(4) the company is held, for 50 per cent or more, under a joint venture arrangement by two or more legal entities which are subject to the structure regime (or mitigated regime) or which are 'dependent' companies of such a legal entity.

Dispensation

A large company may also apply to the Minister of Justice for a dispensation from the provisions (or part thereof) of the structure regime.

1.8   AMENDMENT OF ARTICLES OF ASSOCIATION, CONVERSION AND WINDING-UP OF THE COMPANY

1.8.1   AMENDMENT OF ARTICLES OF ASSOCIATION

Authority

The general meeting of shareholders is exclusively authorised to amend the articles of association. No special majority or quorum is required by law, but the articles of association often provide for this.

The articles of association may make the exclusive authority of the general meeting subject to conditions. Examples of such conditions are:

(1) amendment can only take place upon proposal by the

meeting of priority shareholders or by the managing board; or

(2)   amendment requires prior approval by the supervisory board.

Procedure

Requirements for a valid amendment of the articles of association are:

(1)   a resolution of the general meeting of shareholders;
(2)   a notarial deed of the amendment; and
(3)   a statement of no-objection in respect of the amendment by the Minister of Justice (see also section **1.2.1** under (3)).

Statement of no-objection

One of the grounds on which the Minister of Justice may refuse to issue a statement of no objection is that the amendment *or the manner in which it is effected* is contrary to public policy, statutory law or the articles of association.

The Minister will for instance refuse to approve the amendment if the resolution of the general meeting was passed without the special majority required by the articles of association.

Trade register

A certified copy of the deed of amendment must be filed with the trade register together with the revised text of the articles of association.

Bankruptcy

During bankruptcy of the company the articles of association cannot be amended without the approval of the receiver (*curator*).

1.8.2   CONVERSION

A BV can be converted into an NV and *vice versa*. The conversion will not result in the creation of a new legal entity. The same legal entity will continue to exist but governed by a different regime.

Procedure

To effect a valid conversion there must be:

(1)   a resolution of the general meeting approving the conver-

sion and the related amendment of the articles of association (for amendment, see section **1.8.1**);

(2) a notarial deed for the conversion and the amendment of the articles of association and containing the revised articles;

(3) a statement of no-objection by the Minister of Justice approving the notarial deed;

(4) if a BV is converted into an NV, a balance sheet and a specified accountant's statement (which must be attached to the notarial deed).

Trade register

A certified copy of the notarial deed (and—if applicable—the documents referred to in (4)) must be filed with the trade register.

1.8.3 WINDING UP

General

New provisions in Book 2 Civil Code regarding the winding up of legal entities came into force on 1 January 1992. The new provisions in as far as these are relevant for companies will be summarised in this paragraph.

A company can, *inter alia*, be wound up:

(1) by a resolution of the general meeting of shareholders (NB: authority to resolve this cannot be delegated);

(2) upon the company having been declared bankrupt by (i) termination of the bankruptcy as a result of a lack of assets or (ii) insolvency;

(3) by the courts in a number of specified circumstances provided for in Book 2 Civil Code.

Winding up by the courts

The courts may wind up the company on various grounds, including:

(1) the company's objects are contrary to public policy;

(2) the company's incorporation is defective or its articles of association do not comply with statutory requirements;

(3) the company cannot realise its objects due to a lack of assets or has ceased its activities for the realisation of its objects;

(4) the company violates the prohibitions in Book 2 Civil Code relating to it or violates its articles of association;

(5)   an NV's issued or paid-up capital is below the statutory minimum; a BV's equity is below the required minimum capital and certain other conditions are fulfilled;
(6)   as a measure in connection with an inquiry into the company's affairs (see section **1.9.3**).

Trade register
The winding up must be registered with the trade register.

Liquidation
Upon winding up of the company, the company's property must be liquidated. If there are no assets, no liquidation will take place (and no liquidators are appointed). If there are assets (these do not have to be limited to money), the liquidator(s) will pay the company's creditors and distribute the remainder to the shareholders and other entitled parties in proportion to their respective rights.

If the company is wound up by a resolution of shareholders or by a provision in the articles of association, the managing directors act as liquidators.

In case of dissolution by a court, liquidators are appointed by the same court.

If, to the liquidators' knowledge, there are no assets left in the company, the liquidation will be completed and the company will cease to exist.

1.9   DISPUTES BETWEEN SHAREHOLDERS AND THE RIGHT OF INQUIRY

1.9.1   INTRODUCTION

Dutch company law provides for two procedures through which corporate disputes can be resolved. The first procedure relates to disputes arising from the misconduct of a shareholder and offers the remedies of 'forced transfer' or 'forced acquisition'. The second procedure relates to the request for an inquiry (*enquête*) into the company's policy or conduct of business.

The rules on disputes between shareholders are of a recent date (1989). The right of inquiry is of an earlier date (1971).

1.9.2 DISPUTES BETWEEN SHAREHOLDERS

Applicability

The provisions regarding disputes between shareholders (and the remedies offered) only apply to:

(1) BVs;

(2) NVs, the articles of association of which

(a) only provide for registered shares;

(b) contain restrictions on share transfer; and

(c) do not permit the issue of bearer depositary receipts of shares.

If the articles of association or an agreement provide for another method of resolving disputes between shareholders, a claim for 'forced transfer' or 'forced acquisition' (see below) can in principle not be filed.

Forced transfer of shares

One or more shareholders who, alone or jointly, hold at least one third of the issued capital may seek a court order against another shareholder forcing him to transfer his shares to the claimant(s). The procedure must be based on the ground that the defendant by his conduct prejudices the interests *of the company* to such an extent that the continuation of his shareholding cannot reasonably be tolerated.

If the court decides in favour of the claimant(s), it appoints one or three experts who must report on the price of the shares. The court may at the same time prohibit the defendant from exercising his voting rights. Upon the expert(s) having reported, the court will determine the price of the shares and order the claimant(s) to pay this in cash. Within two weeks after the judgement has been served, the defendant must deliver the shares against payment of the fixed price.

Forced acquisition of shares

The misconduct of one or more shareholders may also lead to a co-shareholder wishing to withdraw as a shareholder. To effect this, such shareholder may seek a court order against his 'misbehaving' co-shareholder(s) to acquire his shares. The ground for such action is that the *claimant's* rights or interests are prejudiced to such an extent that he cannot reasonably be expected to continue his shareholding.

As in the procedure for forced transfer, experts report on the price of the shares, whereupon the Court will determine the price and order the claimant to deliver the shares. Within two weeks after the judgement has been served the defendant(s) must take the shares and pay the fixed price.

Competent Court

Both procedures are brought before the District Court in the district in which the company is established. Appeal is made to the Enterprise Division of the Court of Appeal in Amsterdam (see **Introduction**).

1.9.3 RIGHT OF INQUIRY (*ENQUÊTE*)

Applicability

The provisions regarding the right of inquiry apply to companies, cooperatives and mutual insurance companies. The focus in this paragraph will be on companies.

Procedure

At the request of certain parties, the Enterprise Division of the Court of Appeal in Amsterdam may appoint one or more persons to investigate a company's policy and course of business. The persons entitled to file the request are:

(1) shareholders or holders of depositary receipts, who alone or jointly hold at least 10 per cent of the issued capital or shares in the nominal amount of Dfl 500,000;

(2) trade unions which have members among the employees of the company;

(3) persons who have this right pursuant to the articles of association or an agreement; or

(4) the public prosecutor (*procureur-generaal*) with the Court of Appeal in Amsterdam for reasons of public interest.

Before the request is filed, the requesting party must have informed the company of its objections and must have allowed the company a reasonable period to consider these and take measures.

Decision of the court

The Enterprise Division will decide on the request as soon as possible. The request will only be granted if 'there appear to be well-founded reasons to doubt the correctness of the company's policy'. If the request is granted, the Enterprise Division will appoint one or more investigators and determine the maximum costs of the investigation. These costs are in principle paid by the company.

The investigation may be ordered in respect of the entire policy and business of the company or only part thereof and may be limited to the policy during a certain period. In its decision the Enterprise Division will usually briefly describe the scope of the investigation.

Report

The investigators have access to the company's books and property. Managing and supervisory directors and employees of the company may have to provide information to the investigators.

The outcome of the investigation is included in a report. There is no statutory period within which the report must be completed.

Mismanagement

If it appears from the report that mismanagement (*wanbeleid*) by the company took place, the Enterprise Division may take certain measures against the company (see below). The Enterprise Division may also render a declaratory judgement that mismanagement took place. The fact that mismanagement was established may be relevant for other procedures, for instance a procedure whereby a managing director of the company is held personally liable.

Measures

Provided it is so requested, the Enterprise Division may at its discretion take one or more measures for a certain period of time. Other than in proceedings against the company on the basis of art 26 of the Works Council Act (see section **1.11.4**), the Enterprise Division in inquiry proceedings can take no provisional measures at the start of the proceedings.

The measures in inquiry proceedings can only be taken after 'mismanagement' has been established.

The following measures are available:
(1) suspension or annulment of a resolution of the managing directors, supervisory directors, general meeting of shareholders or any other corporate body of the company;

(2)   suspension or dismissal of one or more managing or supervisory directors;

(3)   temporary appointment of one or more managing or supervisory directors;

(4)   temporary deviation from certain provisions in the articles of association to be specified by the Enterprise Division;

(5)   temporary transfer of shares to a trustee (*ten titel van beheer*); or

(6)   winding up of the company.

1.10   ANNUAL ACCOUNTS AND ANNUAL REPORT

1.10.1   INTRODUCTION

Title 9 of Book 2 Civil Code, implementing the Fourth and Seventh EC Company Law Directives (Official Journal 1978 L222/11 and Official Journal 1983 L193/1), contains detailed provisions on the financial reporting by Dutch companies.

A distinction is made in Title 9 between:

(1)   *the annual accounts*: these accounts, drawn up by the managing board, consist of the balance sheet, the profit and loss statement and the explanatory notes;

(2)   *the annual report*: this is a report by the managing board (usually called the 'management report') regarding the condition of the company at the balance sheet date and the course of business during the past financial year; the report also sets out information on the expected course of business;

(3)   *additional information*: this is the information, listed in art 392 of Title 9 which must be supplemented by the managing board to the annual accounts and the annual report.

Most of the provisions of Title 9 deal with the contents of the annual accounts.

1.10.2   KEY PROVISIONS

Contents

As a general rule, the annual accounts must be prepared in accordance with generally accepted accounting principles and provide such information as to enable the reader to form a sound opinion of the assets and liabilities and the results of the company and, if possible, its solvency and liquidity.

The Fourth and Seventh EC Company Law Directive on the form and content of the annual accounts have been incorporated. Depending on the size of the company, the contents of the annual accounts may vary. 'Small companies' (to a large extent) and 'medium-sized companies' (to a lesser extent) are exempted from including certain items in the accounts.

A company is 'small' or 'medium' if two of these three conditions are met:

(1)   the value of its assets does not exceed Dfl4m or Dfl17m respectively;
(2)   its net turnover does not exceed Dfl8m or Dfl35m respectively;
(3)   the average number of its employees is less than 50 or 250 respectively.

Adoption

The managing board must draw up the annual accounts and make them available for inspection by the shareholders within five months after the end of the company's financial year. The annual accounts are signed by the managing and the supervisory directors. The period of five months can be extended by another six months in special circumstances upon resolution by the general meeting of shareholders.

The annual accounts are adopted by the general meeting of shareholders. In a company to which the 'structure' provisions apply, the supervisory board adopts the annual accounts and the general meeting approves these (see also section **1.7.3**).

Audit and auditor's statement

The company must instruct a chartered accountant to audit the annual accounts. A 'small' company is exempt from this obligation.

As a general rule, the auditor is appointed by the general meeting of shareholders.

The auditor reports on the audit to the managing board and the supervisory board. The auditor furthermore sets out the results of the audit in a separate statement as to whether the annual accounts present a 'true and fair' view.

Publication

The annual accounts of the company together with the annual report and the additional information (this includes the auditor's statement referred to above) must be made public by filing a copy thereof with the trade register. Filing must take place within eight days after the adoption of the accounts or—if the 'structure' regime applies to the company—within eight days after the approval of the accounts.

'Small' companies only have to file a limited balance sheet with explanatory notes.

If no adoption or approval of the annual accounts has taken place within seven months after the end of the financial year, the managing board must proceed to file the annual accounts, stating that these have not yet been adopted or approved.

Group exemption

A company, the financial information of which has been consolidated in the consolidated accounts of a group company (usually the parent), may profit from the group exemption of art 403 of Title 9. If exempt, the company merely has to make up limited annual accounts which do not have to be made public. No audit is required.

The most important conditions for the exemption are:
(1)	the shareholders have agreed to the deviation from the provisions of Title 9;
(2)	the Seventh EC Directive applies to the consolidated accounts of the consolidating group company;
(3)	the consolidating group company has declared in writing that it assumes liability for all debts of the exempt company and this declaration has been filed with the trade register.

1.10.3 LIABILITY AND DISPUTES

Liability

Managing and supervisory directors may be personally liable for misrepresentations in the annual accounts, the annual report and interim statements, provided they were published (see section **1.6.3** and section **1.6.6**). In case of bankruptcy of the company, mismanagement by the managing directors will be presumed to have occurred if the managing board has failed to publish the annual accounts in accordance with the statutory provisions (see also section **1.6.3**).

Disputes

Any 'interested party' can institute proceedings before the Enterprise Division of the Court of Appeal in Amsterdam (see **Introduction**) on the ground that the annual accounts, the annual report or the additional information do not comply with the statutory rules. The accountant who has audited the annual accounts will be heard by the Enterprise Division before a judgement is rendered. If the Enterprise Division decides in favour of the claimant, it will order the company to adjust the annual accounts, the annual report or the additional information in accordance with its instructions. Violation of this order constitutes an economic offence under the Act on Economic Offences.

If the company fails to instruct an auditor or to publish the accounts, any interested party may seek a court order against the company. Such proceedings are conducted before the District Courts in first instance.

1.11   WORKS COUNCIL

1.11.1   INTRODUCTION

Since the first Works Council Act of 1950, employee participation has become an important feature of Dutch company law. By various amendments to the Works Council Act (particularly in 1971 and 1979) the powers of the works council have been substantially increased. The most recent amendment of the Act (January 1990) had the purpose of simplifying the various procedures provided for in the Act.

Scope

The Act relates to employee participation in three types of enterprises:

(1) enterprises with more than 100 employees;
(2) enterprises in which at least 35 persons work more than one third of normal working hours; and
(3) enterprises with 10–35 employees.

There is only very limited employee participation in enterprises referred to in (3).

The 'entrepreneur' who runs an enterprise referred to in (1) or (2) must establish a works council (*ondernemingsraad* or 'OR').

The rights of the '100 plus' works council are somewhat more extensive than the '35–100' works council.

Entrepreneur and enterprise

The 'entrepreneur' within the meaning of the Act is the natural person or legal entity which runs the enterprise. An 'enterprise' is defined as 'each separately operating organisational unit in which work is performed on the basis of employment agreements'. Thus, a company as 'entrepreneur' may run more than one enterprise within the meaning of the Act and may therefore have to establish more than one works council.

1.11.2 JOINT, CENTRAL AND GROUP WORKS COUNCILS

Joint works council

A joint works council may—and sometimes must—be established:

(1) if a company runs two or more enterprises which *together* employ more than 100 (or 35) employees; or

(2) if two or more companies belonging to the same 'group' run two or more enterprises which together employ more than 100 (or 35) employees.

The joint works council will represent all employees in the enterprises concerned.

Central works council

The entrepreneur who has established *two or more* works councils may—and sometimes must—establish a central works council (COR) for the enterprises run by him.

If two or more works councils were established by two or more entrepreneurs who belong to the same group, a central works council may (have to) be established for all enterprises run by these entrepreneurs.

As a general rule, the members of the central works council are elected by the works councils in the various enterprises from their own members.

The central works council will exclusively deal with matters which are of 'joint interest' for all or a majority of the enterprises concerned.

Group works council

The entrepreneur may also establish a group works council

(GOR) for a certain number of his enterprises provided there are two or more works councils within that group.

1.11.3 COMPOSITION AND FUNCTIONING

Composition
   The works council consists exclusively of employees of the enterprise concerned. The number of members of the works council varies between three and 25, depending on the number of employees in the enterprise.

Membership
   As a general rule the term of membership is three years but the works council's regulations (see below) may provide otherwise. The members can be re-elected.
   All persons who have been employed for more than six months have the right to vote in the elections for the works council. Persons who have been employed for more than 12 months can be elected. The election takes place on the basis of lists of candidates. A separate list can be made up for each group of employees or department to effect a proportional representation within the works council.

Organisation and expenses
   The works council will have regulations (*reglement*), *inter alia*, on its own procedure and the delegation of its duties.
   The works council may establish special 'committees' to deal with certain aspects of the works council's duties. The works council may also invite experts to attend a works council meeting.
   Reasonable expenses made by the works council are for the account of the entrepreneur. The entrepreneur and the works council may also agree on a budget for the works council.

Meetings
   The works council holds its meetings as much as possible during working hours. The frequency of the meetings may vary.
   In addition to its own meetings, the works council meets at least six times a year with the entrepreneur (the 'consultation meeting'). In certain circumstances, the Act specifically provides that a consultation meeting must be held. If the entrepreneur is a company, a managing director will usually attend these consultation meetings on its behalf.

Confidentiality

The members of the works council and its committees have a duty to keep confidential all information which has come to their notice in their capacity of member. The entrepreneur may also impose confidentiality on these members in respect of particular matters.

Protection

The entrepreneur must ensure that members or ex-members of the works council or its committees and candidates or ex-candidates in the works council elections are protected against any disadvantage in their position as a result of their works council activities. The same persons cannot be dismissed except in certain circumstances (see further section **2.7** under (3) Dismissal prohibitions).

Rescission of the employment agreement by the Cantonal Court (see section **2.7**) may only take place if the court finds it plausible that there is no connection between the request for rescission and the (ex)membership or candidature.

1.11.4 RIGHTS OF THE WORKS COUNCIL

Rights

A works council has three important rights:

(1) the right to render *advice* on certain proposed decisions which are of an 'economic' nature (art 25);

(2) the right to be asked to *consent* with certain proposed decisions of a 'social' nature (art 27); and

(3) a right to receive all the *information and data* which the works council reasonably requires to perform its task and certain further information and data which are specified by the Act.

Right of advice (art 25)

The works council must be given the opportunity by the entrepreneur to render advice on the following proposed decisions:

(1) to transfer control of the enterprise or part of it;

(2) to acquire or give up control of another enterprise or to enter into, make a major change in or terminate a long-term cooperation with another enterprise;

(3) to terminate the activities of the enterprise or part of it;

(4) to effect an important reduction, extension or other change in the enterprise's activities;
(5) to effect an important change in the organisation of the enterprise or the distribution of powers within the enterprise;
(6) to change the location of the enterprise's activities;
(7) to hire groups of persons to be employed permanently or temporarily;
(8) to make an important investment for the enterprise;
(9) to obtain an important credit facility for the enterprise;
(10) to commission outside consultants in respect of the above mentioned matters.

NB: The 35–100 works council has a right of advice on the same matters but *only if and in so far as* the proposed division may lead to the loss of jobs by—or to a major change in the conditions of employment or the working conditions of—a minimum of one quarter of the work force in the enterprise.

Transfer of control (art 25(a))

The question often arises as to whether the works council of a Dutch company which is the *subject* of an acquisition, has a right of advice in respect of the acquisition. In case of 'legal' merger or a business transfer, the company will be a party to the transaction and the works council will clearly be involved.

If, however, the company is taken over by way of *share purchase*, this is less evident because the decision to transfer the shares will not be taken by the company but by its shareholder(s). In such case, however, it is generally assumed—and this view is supported by case law—that the transfer of shares by the only shareholder, or by a majority shareholder who has actual influence on the company's policy, is a decision on which the works council of the company has a right of advice. The same will apply if the sole or majority shareholder is a foreign company or individual.

NB: A transfer of control as meant here may also result from the transfer by a shareholder of part of his shares.

Appointment or dismissal of directors

The works council, in addition, has a right of advice regarding the proposed appointment or dismissal of *managing directors*. The works council, however, has no right of appeal if the final decision does not conform with its advice; the entrepreneur does not have to suspend his decision (see below).

The works council in a 'large' company has certain rights in connection with the appointment of *supervisory* directors pursuant to the 'structure' provisions of Book 2 Civil Code (see section **1.7.2**).

Procedure

The entrepreneur must ask for advice at such a time as to allow it to have significant influence on the proposed decision.

In connection with the request for advice, certain information must be provided to the works council.

Before the works council renders advice, a consultation meeting with the entrepreneur must be held at least once.

Upon having received the advice of the works council, the entrepreneur must notify the works council of his final decision.

Unless the decision conforms with the works council's advice, the entrepreneur must *suspend* his decision for one month after this notification. The entrepreneur is prohibited from implementing his decision during this period. During this period the works council may appeal from the decision (see below).

NB: This obligation to suspend does not apply in respect of a 35–100 works council.

Appeal

The works council may appeal (on the basis of art 26) to the Enterprise Division of the Court of Appeal in Amsterdam (see **Introduction**) against the entrepreneur's decision:

(1)   if the decision does not conform with the works council's advice;
(2)   if facts or circumstances have emerged which would have resulted in a different advice of the works council had such facts or circumstances been known to it; or
(3)   if the entrepreneur has not asked the works council to render advice although he had an obligation to do so.

The only *ground* for the appeal is that 'the entrepreneur, taking into account all interests concerned, could not reasonably have taken his decision'.

Provisional measures

If the Enterprise Division decides in favour of the works

council it can, upon request, take the following measures against the entrepreneur:

(1) order the entrepreneur to rescind his decision in whole or in part or reverse certain consequences of that decision;

(2) prohibit the entrepreneur from implementing the decision or part thereof.

The same measures may also be taken as provisional measures shortly after the appeal is made.

As it may still take several weeks before a provisional measure can be obtained, the works council can also seek an order against the entrepreneur from the President of the District Court in preliminary relief proceedings (see **Introduction**).

Third party rights

The Act specifically provides that a measure on the basis of art 26, whether provisional or not, cannot affect rights acquired by third parties. However, a third party acting in bad faith, ie a party who knew that the works council's rights were neglected, may not be protected by this provision.

Right of consent (art 27)

A further reaching right of the works council is its right of consent in respect of certain decisions of a 'social' nature.

Such decisions include, *inter alia*, decisions to introduce, amend or withdraw:

(1) pension, profit sharing or saving schemes;

(2) working hours and holiday regulations;

(3) measures relating to safety and health at work;

(4) regulations regarding training of personnel and evaluation of performance.

The decisions must be of a collective nature. If the matter concerned is already provided for in a Collective Bargaining Agreement (see section **2.8**), the works council has no right of consent.

Procedure

A consultation meeting must be held at least once concerning the proposed decision. The works council subsequently informs the entrepreneur as soon as possible of its decision to give consent or not.

If no consent is given, the entrepreneur may ask the

approval of the Cantonal Court (see **Introduction**) to take the proposed decision.

Nullity

A decision as referred to in art 27 of the Act which was taken without the works council's consent or the Cantonal Court's approval, is *void* provided that within a month the works council has invoked, in writing, the nullity against the entrepreneur. If nevertheless the entrepreneur starts implementing the decision, the works council can ask the Cantonal Court to prohibit the entrepreneur to do this.

The entrepreneur, in turn, can ask the Cantonal Court to declare that the works council was unjustified in invoking the nullity.

1.11.5 ACTION FOR COMPLIANCE WITH THE ACT

On the basis of art 36 of the Act, the Cantonal Court can be requested to order the entrepreneur or the works council to comply with the Act.

For instance, each interested party may ask for an order against the entrepreneur to establish a works council or to comply with the provisions regarding the election of works council members. On the basis of the same article, the works council may try to obtain an order against the entrepreneur to ask the works council's advice for a proposed decision of an 'economic' nature (unless an appeal to the Enterprise Division ex art 26 is already pending) or for a proposed decision to appoint or dismiss a managing director.

Before the Cantonal Court considers the request, the claimant must first ask the Enterprise Committee (*Bedrijfscommissie*', see **Introduction**) in the relevant branch of trade or industry to mediate in the dispute.

2
EMPLOYMENT LAW

2.1 INTRODUCTION

Employment law is a complicated area of Dutch law. The following is no more than an outline of the most important aspects of the law relating to employment agreements. The Civil Code contains a far more extensive and detailed regulation of the employment agreement than for most other types of agreement. The other important source of law in respect of individual employment agreements, the collective bargaining agreement, is dealt with in section **2.8**.

A description of the social security system would be beyond the scope of this book. It is, however, important to mention the main social security laws for employees. This is done in the last paragraph of this chapter.

In 1989 a bill was introduced to Parliament to revise the law relating to the termination of employment agreements. At the time of writing it was expected that the new law would come into force in the summer of 1992. In the following paragraphs the changes in the law, such as they affect the subjects dealt with, will be briefly described.

2.2 JURISDICTION IN EMPLOYMENT MATTERS AND APPLICABILITY OF DUTCH LAW TO EMPLOYMENT AGREEMENTS

Cantonal Court

With the exception of disputes relating to the employment of a managing director of a company, disputes relating to employment agreements, collective bargaining agreements and provisions of collective bargaining agreements which have been declared generally applicable, are heard by the Cantonal Court.

Disputes relating to the employment of managing directors are heard by the District Court.

The competent Cantonal Court is the Cantonal Court of the region within which the work is normally carried out or in which the defendant resides or is established. If the work is normally carried out within the regions of more than one Cantonal Court, the employee-plaintiff may start proceedings either before the Cantonal Court of the region in which the employee-plaintiff resides or before the Cantonal Court of the region in which the employer resides or is established.

Disputes relating to the employment of a statutory director of a company are heard by the District Court. The rules of relative competence set out above do not apply to proceedings involving the employment of a managing director of a company.

International jurisdiction

The question of whether the Dutch courts have jurisdiction in matters with international aspects is in the first place answered on the basis of the EC Convention on Jurisdiction and Enforcement in Civil and Commercial Matters of 27 September 1968 (as amended).

The rules of relative competence as set out above are only relevant to determine the international jurisdiction of the Dutch courts if the defendant resides or is established outside the territory of the contracting States or if both parties who have made a choice of jurisdiction reside or are established outside the territory of the contracting States.

Applicable law

As a general rule, Dutch law applies if the employment agreement relates to work carried out in the Netherlands. If an employment agreement has international aspects, eg if the employer resides or is established in a country other than where the employee carries out the work, the question arises as to which law is applicable.

Main rule in case law

The main rule adopted by the Supreme Court before the EC Convention on the law applicable to contractual obligations (see below), which came into force on 1 September 1991, is that if a particular country can be pointed out as the country where the work is (normally) carried out, the employment agreement is governed by the law of that country. If the employee works in more than one country, the applicable law is the law of the country where the employee has his central base of operations. If, however, the employee works in various different countries but has no central base of operations, the law of the country where the employer resides or is established will apply to the employment agreement.

Exceptions

There are exceptions to these rules. Special circumstances may lead to applicability of yet another legal system. The Supreme Court has for example decided that if an employer sends an employee abroad who initially worked in the country where the employer resides or is established, the employment agreement will normally continue to be governed by the law of the country where the employer resides or is established.

Choice of law

The question arises as to whether—and if so, to what extent—the parties to an employment agreement may choose the law which applies to their relationship. The possibility of making a choice of law has been accepted by the Supreme Court. However, this choice of law, especially to the extent that a legal system other than the Dutch would apply, is only possible if there are connecting factors to the chosen law.

EC Convention on the law applicable to contractual obligations

The rules developed in Dutch case law are to a great extent in accordance with the provisions of the EC Convention on the law applicable to contractual obligations of 19 June 1980.

Article 6 of the convention provides that an employment agreement, in the absence of a choice of law by the parties, is governed:

   ...   (a)   by the law of the country in which the employee habitually carries out his work in performance of the contract, even if he is temporarily employed in another country; or

         (b)   if the employee does not habitually carry out his work in any one country, by the law of the country in which the place of business through which he was engaged, is situated;...

The convention leaves open the possibility of special circumstances from which it appears that the employment agreement is more closely connected with another country, in which case the law of that country applies.

A choice of law may not have as a result that the employee is deprived of the protection afforded to him by the mandatory rules of the law which would in the absence of choice be applicable.

Decree on Labour Relations 1945

The Decree on Labour Relations 1945 (*Buitengewoon besluit arbeidsverhoudingen 1945*) prohibits the termination of an employment agreement without the consent of the Minister of Social Affairs and Employment, who has delegated the authority to grant dismissal licences to the Regional Directors for Employment Policy (see section 2.7). It is important to establish whether this Decree applies to an employment agreement which has international aspects. The Supreme Court has held that the decisive criterion for the applicability of the Decree on Labour Relations 1945 is whether interests of the Dutch labour market are involved in employment agreements under which the work is carried out outside the Netherlands. The Supreme Court has also held that applicability of the Decree depends on the fulfilment of the conditions which are contained in the Decree's own 'scope rule'. The employment agreement being governed by Dutch law is not one of these conditions.

Act on minimum wages and minimum holiday allowance

The Act on minimum wages and minimum holiday allowance (*Wet minimum loon en minimum vakantiebijslag*) contains a provision on its applicability to employment agreements with international aspects. If the work is carried out in the Netherlands, the Act applies. The Act also applies if the work is not carried out in the Netherlands, but both the employee and the employer reside or are established in the Netherlands. An employer with a permanent establishment in the Netherlands for the carrying on of his profession or trade or with a permanent representative in the Netherlands is deemed to be resident of or established in the Netherlands.

2.3 EMPLOYMENT AGREEMENTS; GENERAL

Form

Like most agreements under Dutch law, the employment agreement is not subject to any conditions of form. An employment agreement may therefore be concluded orally. However, certain provisions such as a non-competition provision are only valid if made in writing. Obviously, a contract signed by both parties or an exchange of letters is the best evidence of the employment agreement which the parties have entered into.

Term

An employment agreement may be entered into for a fixed term or for an indefinite period of time. If no fixed duration has been agreed, the employment agreement is deemed to be for an indefinite period of time. An employment agreement for a fixed term, which may not be terminated unilaterally by either one of the parties before the expiration of the term, unless otherwise agreed, terminates automatically upon expiration of the agreed term, but may be renewed. Renewal may be expressly agreed or may be implied. Unless otherwise agreed, renewal takes place under the same terms and conditions. The law provides that if the employment is continued without objection, the employment is considered to have been renewed for the same term (though for one year at the most) and under the previous terms and conditions. A collective bargaining agreement may, however, provide for implied renewal for an indefinite period of time. For termination of a renewed employment agreement a dismissal licence and the giving of notice is required.

After the amendments to the law relating to termination of employment agreements (see section **2.1**) have come into force, it will be explicitly provided in the Civil Code that an employment agreement for a fixed term may only be terminated by giving notice before the expiration of the term, if for each of the parties this right has been agreed to in writing. Under the new law continuation by the parties without objection of an employment agreement for a fixed term will no longer lead to the employment being considered renewed for the same term with a maximum of one year. Instead, it will be considered renewed on the same terms and conditions for an indefinite period of time and it will therefore become subject to the rules for termination of employment agreements of that category. An employment agreement for an indefinite period of time or for a fixed term may only be renewed for a fixed term, if such renewal is agreed to in writing.

If an employment agreement is renewed for a fixed term, it will be necessary to give notice (on the basis of a dismissal licence) in order for it to be terminated. However, this does not apply if it concerns a first renewal by no more than six months and the parties have agreed in writing that the employment will terminate upon expiration of the fixed term without the giving of notice being required.

A collective bargaining agreement (or a regulation from a competent public authority) may contain rules that deviate from these provisions.

Trial period

The parties may include a provision for a trial period in the employment agreement. As a general rule, a trial period may only be validly agreed upon at the very beginning of an employment relationship. To be valid, the trial period provision must comply with the following requirements:

(1) the trial period must be the same for both parties;
(2) the trial period may not be longer than two months;
(3) a new trial period following a lapsed trial period may only be agreed upon if the total duration of the trial periods does not exceed the maximum of two months.

If these requirements are not met, the whole trial period provision is void. A trial period exceeding two months will not be deemed to be a (valid) trial period for two months.

During the trial period each of the parties may terminate the employment agreement without giving notice and without complying with the statutory provisions which are applicable to termination by the giving of notice (see section **2.7**). This means that the provisions on notice periods and the dismissal prohibitions do not apply. The provisions of the Decree on Labour Relations 1945 do not apply to termination during the trial period. Termination during the trial period also cannot give rise to a claim for 'apparently unreasonable' dismissal (see section **2.7**).

Under the new law it will no longer be possible to include a trial period in an employment agreement which is entered into for a fixed term of less than one year. It will also be explicitly provided that a trial period may only be agreed to if it does not concern the renewal (whether for an indefinite period of time or for a fixed term) of an employment agreement. It will become possible that in a collective bargaining agreement (or a regulation from a competent public authority) the Civil Code provisions relating to a trial period (except the provision on the maximum length of the trial period) are deviated from.

Amendment

An employment agreement may be amended; for instance wages, additional benefits or working hours may be changed. This requires the consent from both parties unless—pursuant to the agreement—one of the parties is entitled to amend the agreement unilaterally. Generally, unilateral amendment is only possible if it has been expressly agreed to. In any event, the exercise of the power to amend the employment agreement unilaterally is subject to the requirements of reasonableness and fairness. Unilateral amendment of provisions in the employment agreement, the amendment of which has not been expressly provided for, is, in general, not possible. Special circumstances may, however, lead to it being unreasonable for the employee to demand the continuing performance of a certain provision in the agreement.

Transition

To implement EC Directive 77/187 of 14 February 1977 (Official Journal of the EC of 5 March 1977 L61/26), arts 1639aa–dd have been included in the Civil Code. They provide for transition of employment agreements by operation of law upon transfer of an enterprise or part of it pursuant to an agreement—*inter alia* and in practice most important—for the sale and purchase of the enterprise. The acquirer of the enterprise assumes the rights and obligations of the transferor under the existing employment agreements. The employees become employees of the acquirer and their conditions of employment remain the same, with the exception of certain pension rights and rights under certain savings schemes. For one year after the transfer, transferor and acquirer are jointly and severally liable for the fulfilment of obligations under employment agreements that have occurred before the transfer.

'Enterprise' means an organisation for the manufacturing or delivery of goods or the rendering of services (which includes a non-profit organisation).

The provisions of articles 1639aa–dd do not apply to the transfer of an enterprise by the receiver in bankruptcy (*faillissement*), but do apply to transfer during temporary moratorium of payment (*surséance van betaling*).

2.4 WAGES AND EMPLOYMENT CONDITIONS

General

In principle, the parties to an employment agreement are free to determine the wages. This freedom of the parties is, however, to a certain extent limited by the provisions of the Act on minimum wages and minimum holiday allowance, art 1637ij of the Civil Code and the Act on equal treatment of men and women (*Wet gelijke behandeling van mannen en vrouwen*).

The parties may determine wages in their individual employment agreement. Often, however, wages are determined in a collective bargaining agreement.

Minimum wages

According to the Act on minimum wages and minimum holiday allowance an employee who is between 23 and 65 years of age is entitled to minimum wages determined by the Minister of Social Affairs and Employment.

Minimum wages for employees under the age of 23 are provided for in a royal decree based on the Act.

These statutory provisions regarding minimum wages are of a mandatory nature and the Act provides that any stipulations which violate such statutory provisions are null and void.

Equal treatment

Article 1637ij of the Civil Code provides that the employer may not distinguish between men and women as regards employment conditions. In respect of wages this is elaborated in the Act on equal treatment of men and women. This Act substantially provides that the wages of a particular employee must be equal to those paid to an employee of the other sex for the same work. Under the Act a committee has been formed which may investigate whether in a particular enterprise distinctions are made between men and women as prohibited by art 1637ij of the Civil Code.

Trade unions may ask the competent court to declare a certain course of action unlawful because of violation of art 1637ij of the Civil Code or claim for an injunction to prohibit such course of action and/or to undo its consequences. The principle of equal payment to male and female employees is also set out in art 119 of the EC Treaty.

Article 1637ij also provides—*inter alia*—that it is prohibited to distinguish between married and unmarried employees as regards the entering into and the termination of employment agreements (see also section **2.7.3**).

'No work, no wages'; exceptions

Wages are not due over the period during which the employee has not carried out work ('no work, no wages'). There are a few exceptions to this rule. One of the most important exceptions is that the employee remains entitled to payment of his wages for a—in the words of the relevant article in the Civil Code—'relatively' short period of time when he is prevented from working through illness or accident.

Employees are very often entitled to payment of their full net wages for a longer period. Any payments of benefits which the employee receives pursuant to social security legislation (which will be briefly discussed below; see section **2.9**) or pursuant to any insurance or from any fund, participation in which is stipulated in or follows from the employment agreement, are deducted from the wages paid during illness.

Another important exception is that the employee remains entitled to payment of his wages if he is prepared to carry out the work but the employer does not let him do so through the employer's own fault or because of an accidental personal inability of the employer.

This exception is especially important in cases of void dismissal (eg the employer has terminated the employment agreement with immediate effect for an 'urgent reason' (see section **2.7**) and the employee has successfully contested his dismissal). The employee's claim for payment of his wages may, however, be mitigated by the court.

Minimum holiday allowance

Employees are entitled to a minimum holiday allowance of 8 per cent of their gross annual wages (including the benefits to which they are entitled on the basis of the Sickness Benefits Act (*Ziektewet*) and the Unemployment Act (*Werkloosheidswet*) (see section **2.9**)). However, to determine the amount of the holiday allowance, the amount by which the wages exceed three times the statutory minimum wages is not taken into account. Collective bargaining agreements may provide for higher amounts of holiday allowance and may even—subject to certain statutory restrictions—provide that there is no entitlement to a holiday allowance or to a lower percentage than 8 per cent.

Additional benefits

Employment agreements often entitle employees to additional benefits such as profit sharing, participation in a share option scheme, payment of 'thirteenth month' wages and payment of a performance bonus.

Working hours

The legislation on working hours and working conditions based on the Labour Act 1919 (*Arbeidswet 1919*), is extensive and complicated. To deal with this aspect of Dutch employment law would go beyond the scope of this book. Only a few general remarks will be made.

The average number of working hours per week in most sectors of industry is 38. This depends on the relevant provisions of the applicable collective bargaining agreement or individual employment agreement.

Working conditions

The Labour Act 1919 further contains provisions relating to rest periods, shift work, overtime and other working conditions; special provisions apply to minors (persons below the age of 18). All of these subjects are usually further elaborated in collective bargaining agreements.

Holidays

Articles 1638bb–mm of the Civil Code contain detailed provisions relating to the employee's holiday entitlement and the employee's right to exercise it.

The number of days per year to which the employee is

entitled is four times the number of working days per week. The parties may agree on a more generous holiday entitlement. Often, collective bargaining agreements provide for more days than the statutory minimum number. An agreement on a smaller number of days is invalid.

The employee has the right to have his holiday for two successive weeks or, if necessary because of the conduct of the employer's business or if the employee so wishes, twice for one week. The holiday weeks must, if possible, begin in the period between 30 April and 1 October. The employer must consult with the employee about the beginning and end of the holiday entitlement when there is no provision for that in the contract or in the applicable collective bargaining agreement.

Holidays cannot be replaced by payment of an amount of money. However, upon the termination of the employment agreement the employee is entitled to payment of his salary over the outstanding days which he has not taken up.

Safety and health

The Working Conditions Act 1980 (*Arbeidsomstandigheden-wet 1980*)—as amended—requires employers to focus their enterprise policies on the protection and improvement of the safety, health and well-being of the employees. The Act contains strict rules on employee safety and authorises the Regional Labour Inspector to issue detailed instructions. Violations of such rules and instructions are punishable by criminal penalties.

2.5 CERTAIN SPECIAL PROVISIONS IN EMPLOYMENT AGREEMENTS

Non-competition/restraint of trade

An employment agreement may contain a provision which imposes restrictions on the freedom of the employee to carry out work, as employee or otherwise, 'in a particular way' after the employment agreement has been terminated (art 1637x of the Civil Code). 'In a particular way' refers to the nature of the work as well as to the time period for which the provision is made and the geographical limits within which the provision applies.

To be valid, a non-competition provision must be made in writing. It does not have to be included in the employment contract, but may be made at any time. Decisive is a written statement from the employee that he agrees to being bound by the non-competition provision; the employer may accept such statement orally.

It is not possible to impose a non-competition restriction on an employee who is under 18 years of age.

Article 1637x of the Civil Code does not apply to provisions which prohibit the employee from having a financial interest in a particular enterprise or in a particular type of enterprise.

Setting aside by the court

The court may at any time set aside a non-competition provision, either wholly or partly, on the ground that the employee is unreasonably injured by it and this bears no relation to the interests of the employer.

The importance for the employer of compliance with the non-competition provision seems to be one of the most important criteria that are applied in case law. Often, the time period and geographical area are limited by the court because of lack of importance of the relevant restrictions for the employer. The position and salary of the employee are also taken into account.

Compensation

The court may further decide that the employer has to pay compensation to the employee for the time during which the employee is (considerably) restricted from carrying out work other than in the employment of the employer. Compensation does not have to be paid if the employee is liable to pay damages to the employer because the employee has not observed the notice period.

Damages

If the employee does not comply with the non-competition provision, the employer may claim for damages. Because it will be difficult to determine the real damages suffered by the employer, the employer's entitlement to damages is often fixed, either at one amount or at a particular amount for each act which contravenes the non-competition provision. The court may mitigate such agreed amount.

The employer who is liable to pay damages to the employee because of the way the employment agreement has been terminated, cannot derive any rights from the non-competition provision. 'Apparently unreasonable' termination of the employment agreement by the employer or rescission by the court because of a change of circumstances (see section **2.7**), however, do not prevent the employer from invoking a non-competition provision.

Intellectual property

An employment agreement may contain provisions on the ownership of intellectual property rights. The Copyright Act (*Auteurswet*) and the Patent Act (*Rijksoctrooiwet*) also contain provisions on employers' and employees' rights. This subject is discussed in Chapter 6.

Confidentiality

It is a criminal offence for an employee to disclose any confidential information about his employer's enterprise during or after his employment. Employment agreements often provide what kind of information is to be kept confidential and to whom it may not be disclosed.

Penalty provisions

The Civil Code contains rules on the penalty as disciplinary measure which may be taken if the employee does not fulfil one of his obligations. The penalty must be based on a written agreement between employer and employee or on employment regulations (*arbeidsreglement*). The possibility of imposing a penalty may also be based on a collective bargaining agreement. A penalty must be distinguished from a fixed amount of damages.

It must be explicitly provided in the contract in respect of which obligations the penalty applies. The purpose towards which the amount of the penalty is applied must also be explicitly referred to in the contract. The penalty may not be for the benefit of the employer or the person who, pursuant to the contract, is entitled to impose the penalty. Within a period of a week no penalty may be imposed upon an employee which exceeds the employee's wages in respect of half a working day.

Stipulations contrary to the above rules are null and void. However, it is possible to deviate from the provisions on the purpose of the penalty in contracts with an employee whose daily wages exceed the amount of the minimum daily wages determined pursuant to the Act on Disability Insurance (*Wet op de arbeidsongeschiktheidsverzekering*) (see section **2.9**).

2.6   SUSPENSION

Suspension (*schorsing*) is not provided for in statutory law. Suspension is allowed if the employer has serious suspicions that there is an 'urgent reason' to terminate the employment agreement but further investigations have to take place. An employee may also be suspended during termination proceedings if the presence of the employee at work is no longer desirable.

If the suspension is not based on a reasonable ground the court may lift it. Usually, an employee turns to the President of the District Court in preliminary relief proceedings. The courts tend to apply rather strict standards in determining whether a suspension is based on a reasonable ground.

Collective bargaining agreements often contain regulations on suspension as a disciplinary measure. In such regulations it is usually provided that suspension may only take place for a limited period of time.

During suspension the employee generally remains entitled to wages.

2.7   TERMINATION OF EMPLOYMENT AGREEMENTS

2.7.1   GENERAL

One of the most important areas of Dutch employment law, which particularly shows the emphasis on protection of the employee's rights and interests, is formed by the rules on termination of the employment agreement.

The Civil Code contains detailed provisions on the various ways in which the employment agreement may terminate. As mentioned in section **2.1**, fairly substantial changes will come into force in the summer of 1992. They will be set out below.

A very important rule is the prohibition of the Decree on Labour Relations 1945, to terminate the employment agreement unilaterally without having obtained prior consent in the form of a dismissal licence from the Regional Director for Employment Policy.

The Act on notification of collective dismissals (*Wet melding collectief ontslag*) requires the employer who intends to terminate the employment of at least 20 of his employees at one or more dates within a period of three months, to notify the 'interested trade unions' and the Regional Director for Employment Policy.

Collective bargaining agreements may give additional rules on termination of employment agreements.

As will be discussed below, the employer who terminates the employment agreement may in some circumstances be liable for severance payments.

2.7.2 FIXED TERM AGREEMENTS

As already discussed (see section **2.3**), an employment agreement for a fixed period of time terminates upon the expiration of the agreed period, unless agreed otherwise. It cannot be terminated unilaterally before that time. However, it may be terminated earlier:

(1) by mutual consent;
(2) during the trial period;
(3) for an 'urgent reason';
(4) by 'rescission' by the Cantonal Court; or
(5) if this has been expressly agreed.

It is not necessary to fix the term of the employment by referring to a particular date. The fixed period may also be defined by reference to the occurrence of certain circumstances, eg completion of a certain defined task. It is, however, not possible to provide that the employment will terminate because of the employee's marriage, illness, pregnancy or military service. In these circumstances termination of the employment agreement by giving the employee notice is prohibited. This will be further discussed below.

2.7.3 AGREEMENTS FOR INDEFINITE PERIOD OF TIME

An employment agreement for an indefinite period of time may be terminated:

(1) by mutual consent;
(2) by giving notice to the other party
  (a) on the basis of a dismissal licence granted by the Regional Director for Employment Policy; and
  (b) with due observance of the relevant notice period;
(3) during the trial period;

(4)   for an 'urgent reason';
(5)   by a 'rescission' by the Cantonal Court; or
(6)   by a combination of alternatives (1) and (5).

Termination by mutual consent

An employee who has agreed to the termination of his employment could possibly forfeit his unemployment benefits under the relevant social security legislation. Therefore, termination of the employment agreement by mutual consent in practice only takes place when the employee wishes to terminate because he wants to change jobs and the employer feels that it would be unreasonable to oppose termination, or when the employer wishes to terminate the employment agreement and the employee agrees because he has already found or expects to find a new job shortly. In the latter type of circumstances the employee may in addition be entitled to a severance payment.

In view of the financial risks for the employee when he agrees to termination of his employment, such agreement must be explicit and unequivocal. It should preferably be confirmed in writing. The employer has a responsibility to ensure that the employee understands the consequences of his agreement to termination.

Termination by giving notice; dismissal licence

Under the new law it will be explicitly provided that the party who wishes to terminate the employment by giving notice must at the request of the other party state the reason for such termination in writing. The Decree on Labour Relations 1945 prohibits the termination of employment without having obtained the consent of the Minister of Social Affairs and Employment. This prohibition applies to the employer and to the employee; however, only termination by the employer will be dealt with, as under the new law the Decree will provide that the prohibition only applies to the employer. The Minister of Social Affairs and Employment has delegated the authority to grant dismissal licences to the Regional Directors for Employment Policy ('Regional Directors'). In the printing industry the authority to grant dismissal licences rests with the Central Bureau for the Printing Industry.

Exceptions

There are three situations in which the prohibition does not apply:

(a) the employment agreement is terminated because of an 'urgent reason', see below;

(b) the employment agreement is terminated by mutual consent, see above;

(c) the employment agreement is terminated as a result of the employer's bankruptcy; the receiver in bankruptcy does not have to obtain a licence from the Regional Director to terminate employment agreements even when this involves employees who have been kept in employment by the receiver during the bankruptcy.

Exempt categories of employees

The Decree on Labour Relations 1945 does not apply to employment relationships with the following categories of employees:

(a) employees of (semi-) governmental bodies (including embassies of foreign states);

(b) teachers;

(c) clerical staff;

(d) employees who, usually for less than three days a week, exclusively or mainly work in a natural person's household.

The Minister of Social Affairs has exempted the employment of statutory directors of NVs and BVs from the prohibition of the Decree.

Rescission by the court

The Decree on Labour Relations 1945 does not affect the possibility that an employment agreement is rescinded by the court because of 'important reasons' or breach of contract.

Procedure

The employer who wishes to terminate the employment of an employee must inform the employee concerned. The employer must file a written application with the Regional Director for the necessary dismissal licence. Generally, the competent authority is the Regional Director of the region in which the employee carries out (or has carried out) his work. The employer has to state the personal data (name, address, age, date of the beginning of the employment, current job and salary) of the employee he wishes to dismiss. He must also explain the reasons for dismissal and submit any written material which may support his application.

The Regional Director then sends a copy of the application to the employee concerned. The employee is normally allowed approximately two weeks to respond in writing to the employer's request. In turn, the employer is allowed approximately two weeks to comment in writing on the employee's reaction. Finally, the employee may make comments in writing on the employer's second submission. The relevant paper work is then handed over to an advisory committee consisting of representatives of employers' associations and trade unions which will advise on the dismissal. Usually, the Regional Director follows the committee's advice.

Valid reason

The employer must prove that he has a valid reason for terminating the employment. This may be lack of performance by the employee or the need to reduce the number of employees for economic reasons.

The Regional Director must be convinced that the termination is socially justified, taking into account the possibilities and interests of the employer and the employee. If the application is based on economic grounds, the Regional Director will grant a dismissal licence provided that the 'seniority principle' (the 'last in first out' rule) is observed. If the application for a dismissal licence is based on the employee's insufficient compliance with the job requirements, the Regional Director will only grant a dismissal licence if:

    (a)   the employer has shown that the employee is not fit for his job;

    (b)   this is not caused by illness or disability of the employee, unless it cannot reasonably be expected from the employer to create suitable work for that employee;

    (c)   the employer has had sufficient contact with the employee to try and procure improvement; and

    (d)   the non-performance of the employee is not caused by

insufficient care for working conditions by the employer.

It is sometimes recommendable that payment of a certain compensation is already offered to the employee concerned in the application for the dismissal licence.

Time frame

The time needed to obtain a decision from the Regional Director is supposed to be between four and six weeks, but in practice this may vary between approximately six weeks and three months and it may even take longer than that.

Recourse

Appeal from decisions of the Regional Director is not possible. If a licence is not granted, the employer may only file a new application if he can submit grounds which have not already been considered in connection with the first application. An employee who has been dismissed on the basis of a dismissal licence has no other recourse than to attempt to have his employment reinstated by the Cantonal Court on the ground that the termination of his employment was 'apparently unreasonable' but such proceedings are hardly ever successful. However, the employer may be required to pay damages to the employee.

Dismissal; giving notice

The dismissal licence specifies the period of time during which it may be used by the employer. This period may not be longer than two months.

After having obtained the dismissal licence the employer must still give notice of termination to the employee and he must do so within the time limit specified in the licence and with due observance of the relevant notice period.

Nullity

If the employment agreement is terminated without the required dismissal licence having been obtained, the employee may invoke the nullity of the termination within six months after he has been informed of the termination. Under the new law the nullity must be invoked within two months. The statute of limitations of any claim in connection with the invoking of the nullity is, however, six months.

Notice period

The notice period to be observed is the longer of:

(a)   the notice period provided for in the individual employment agreement (which may not exceed six months and which may not be shorter for the employee than for the employer); and

(b)   the notice period provided for in the Civil Code.

Notice to be observed by employer

The notice period of the Civil Code to be observed by the employer is:

(a)   one week for each full year of employment since the age of 18 with a minimum equal to the normal period for payment of wages (usually a month) and a maximum of 13 weeks; plus

(b)   one week for each year of employment after the employee has reached the age of 45, again with a maximum of 13 weeks.

There is a minimum of three weeks for employees who are 50 years of age and older and who have been employed for at least one year.

Under the new law the notice period to be observed by the employer is no longer related to the age of the employee but only to the length of service; the notice period is:

(a)   one month, if the employment has lasted for less than five years;

(b)   two months, if the employment has lasted for more than five but less than ten years;

(c)   three months, if the employment has lasted for more than ten but less than fifteen years;

(d)   four months, if the employment has lasted for more than fifteen years.

A shorter notice period than would otherwise apply may only be provided for in a collective bargaining agreement (or in a regulation issued by a competent public authority). It is possible to agree to a longer notice period than would otherwise apply; such agreement must be in writing.

Notice to be observed by employee

The notice period to be observed by the employee is one week for each period of two years of employment since the age of

18 with a minimum of the payment period and a maximum of six weeks.

Under the new law the employee must observe a notice period of one month, unless otherwise agreed in writing.

If the notice period is extended, it may for the employee not exceed six months and for the employer it may not be shorter than twice the length of the period which the employee must observe.

End of notice period

Other than the present law, the new law provides that notice must be given with effect from the end of the calendar month (unless another effective day has been agreed to or is determined by custom). However, under the present law—providing that notice may only be given with effect from the day determined by agreement or custom, or, in the absence of such determination, with effect from any day—it is already customary to extend a notice period to the end of the calendar month.

The end of the notice period must correspond with local customs. In practice, this means that the notice period is extended to the end of the calendar month during which it would otherwise have expired.

The employment terminates after the expiration of the notice period. At that time the entitlement of the employee to payment of wages and other remunerations and his obligation to continue his work will cease. In practice, however, the parties often agree that this period is used by the employee to enjoy the remainder of his holidays or that the employee will simply stay home on full pay.

Irregular termination

If the applicable notice period or the requirements on the effective date of the termination are not complied with, the termination is irregular. Irregular termination entitles the employee to receive statutory damages or compensation for the real damages incurred. The statutory damages are equal to the amount of the employee's wages for the remaining number of days that regular notice would have required. An employee whose employment has been terminated irregularly may also request reinstatement of his employment agreement by the Cantonal Court. This does not apply to a statutory director of a company. A claim for reinstatement of the employment agreement is often converted into a claim for damages. These actions may only be brought during six months following effective termination.

Dismissal prohibitions

A dismissal licence will normally not be granted and can, if granted, in any event not lead to a valid termination of the employment agreement:

(a) if the termination is based on the employee's marriage;

(b) if the termination—that is the legal act of giving notice of termination upon receipt of the dismissal licence—takes place during the employee's sick leave, unless the illness has continued uninterrupted for at least two years;

(c) if the termination takes place during the employee's maternity leave or, if the employee has resumed her work after having given birth, between the seventh and twelfth week after childbirth; under the new law this is related to the ('flexible') period of maternity leave;

(d) if the employee is performing military service;

(e) if the employee is a member of the Works Council or one of its committees, unless:

    (i) the employee has agreed in writing to the termination; or

    (ii) because the business of the employer is being closed down; or

(f) if the employee is a candidate for election to the Works Council or has been a member of the Works Council in the past two years or of one of its committees and the termination takes place without the special permission of the Cantonal Court, unless:

    (i) the employee agrees in writing to the termination; or

    (ii) because the business of the employer is being closed down; or

(g) if the termination would take place because of the employee's membership of a trade union or because of the employee's performance of or participation in trade union activities, unless such activities take place during working hours without the employer's approval (new law).

There are a few other dismissal prohibitions, but they fall outside the scope of this book.

The employer's right to apply for dismissal licences may also be temporarily suspended by the provisions of the Act on notification of collective dismissals or by the provisions of the Works Council Act (*Wet op de ondernemingsraden*).

Nullity

If notice of termination has been given in the circumstances described above the employee may invoke the nullity of the notice by simple letter during a period of two months following notice. If the court decides that the dismissal is 'apparently unreasonable' the employee may claim for—usually substantial—damages.

'Apparently unreasonable' dismissal

If the employer dismisses the employee in an 'apparently unreasonable' way, the court may order the employer to pay compensation. One of the grounds on which a dismissal can be held apparently unreasonable is that the (financial) consequences of the dismissal for the employee are too serious in relation to the interests of the employer.

The amount of compensation to be paid depends on the circumstances of the case, eg the age of the employee, the wages and the duration of the employment as well as (the soundness of) the reasons put forward to justify the dismissal.

Even if the Regional Director has granted a dismissal licence the court may decide that the dismissal is 'apparently unreasonable'.

Instead of compensation, an employee may also request reinstatement of his employment agreement. However, reinstatement is only granted in exceptional circumstances, and the obligation to reinstate can always be 'bought off'.

A claim for compensation on the grounds of an 'apparently unreasonable' dismissal must be filed within six months after the dismissal.

Termination during the trial period

Reference is made to section **2.3**.

Termination for an 'urgent reason'

There may be a situation in which a party to an employment agreement cannot reasonably be expected to continue the employment relationship. If this is caused by the other party, the employment agreement may be terminated without giving notice to the other party and with immediate effect. A dismissal licence is not required and dismissal prohibitions do not apply. Both parties to an employment agreement have the right to terminate the employment relationship for an 'urgent reason', but in practice employees hardly ever terminate their employment agreements for an 'urgent reason'. Therefore termination for an 'urgent reason' by an employee will not be further dealt with.

'Urgent reasons'

A few examples of 'urgent reasons' listed by art 1639p of the Civil Code:

(a)   upon his application for employment the employee has misled the employer by producing false or falsified references or the employee has provided false information to the employer about the way in which his previous employment has ended;

(b)   the employee seriously lacks capability or suitability for the work which he has undertaken to carry out;

(c)   the employee has committed theft, fraud or other crimes involving a breach of trust;

(d)   the employee has inflicted serious bodily harm to the employer, members of his family, relatives or other employees;

(e)   the employee has intentionally damaged the employer's property;

(f)   the employee has disclosed trade or professional secrets;

(g)   the employee has been grossly negligent in the performance of his duties.

Although the examples in the Civil Code will normally constitute 'urgent reasons', this will not necessarily be the case. There may of course also be other circumstances than those listed above that could constitute 'urgent reasons'.

Material; immediate communication

The 'urgent reason' must be material and must be communicated to the employee immediately. A brief delay, for instance to consult a lawyer, has been accepted in case law, but generally delay in terminating the employment agreement after an 'urgent reason' has occurred will be regarded as showing that the reason was not urgent.

Burden of proof

If the employee contests the termination of his employment agreement in court, the employer must prove that he had an 'urgent reason' to terminate the employment agreement.

Nullity

If the reason was not serious and urgent enough to justify an immediate and irrevocable termination, the termination may be declared void. Since no dismissal licence was obtained by the employer, the employee will be entitled to receive his salary over the period from the void termination until the employment agreement is lawfully terminated by obtaining a dismissal licence and with due observance of the relevant notice period. The employee must invoke the nullity of the termination within six months from the date of termination.

Rescission by the Cantonal Court

Instead of filing an application for a dismissal licence, an employer who wishes to terminate the employment of one of his employees may also file a petition with the Cantonal Court for rescission of the employment agreement.

The alternative of termination through rescission proceedings before the Cantonal Court is also available when an application for a dismissal licence has been rejected.

Obviously, 'rescission' proceedings may also be initiated by an employee.

Grounds for rescission

An employment agreement may be rescinded on one of the following grounds:

(a) such behaviour of the other party as would have warranted a termination of his employment with

immediate effect for an 'urgent reason'; or
(b)   'changed circumstances of such nature that the
       employment agreement should reasonably come to an
       end immediately or within a short period of time'.

'Changed circumstances' are generally considered to cover
all conceivable grounds for termination. Although a Cantonal
Court may reject a petition for rescission because of lack of
evidence or because termination is not reasonable in the given
circumstances, a petition is hardly ever rejected on the technical
ground that the facts submitted to the court as the basis of the
petition do not constitute 'changed circumstances' within the
meaning of the law.

Under the new law it will be provided that the Cantonal
Court may only grant a petition for rescission after it has satisfied
itself as to whether the petition is related to the existence in the
relevant case of a dismissal prohibition. 'Dismissal prohibitions'
in this context means:

(a)   the dismissal prohibitions discussed in one of the
       previous paragraphs of this section **2.7.3**;
(b)   the prohibition of art 1637ij of the Civil Code (see also
       section **2.4**), which not only provides that an employer
       may not distinguish between men and women as
       regards employment conditions, but also that discrimi-
       nation is prohibited on the point of termination of
       employment agreements;
(c)   the prohibition contained in the new art 1637ija which
       provides that the conditions subject to which an
       employment agreement is entered into, renewed or
       terminated may not be less favourable for an employee
       who does not have Dutch nationality (but resides in the
       Netherlands) than for an employee with Dutch natio-
       nality; termination in breach of this article or because
       of the employee's invoking this article, is null and void
       (the same sanction applies to breach of art 1637ij).

No appeal

There is no appeal from decisions of the Cantonal Court on
petitions for rescission. Under the new law it will be possible to
appeal with the District Court from the decision of the Cantonal
Court to the extent it relates to the compensation payable. Appeal

from the decision of the District Court may be lodged in cassation proceedings before the Supreme Court.

Compensation

At its discretion the Cantonal Court may decide that the petition will be granted if one party pays a certain compensation, specified in the decision, to the other. Normally, the party which is to pay the compensation is allowed a period of two weeks to withdraw the petition if the amount of the compensation is considered too high.

Guidelines for compensation

Rough guidelines to determine the amount of compensation often applied by Cantonal Courts are:

(a) (i)   one month's salary per year of service for employees under 40;

(ii) one and a half months' salary per year of service for employees who are approximately 45 years of age;

(iii) two months' salary per year of service for employees who are approximately 50 years of age; and

(b) one month's salary for each year of service before the age of 40 was reached and two months' salary for each year of service after the age of 40 was reached.

These are no more than rough guidelines. The amount of compensation is dependent on all circumstances of the matter. Other factors of importance are the extent to which the employer or employee can be blamed, the employer's financial position and the chances for the employee of finding a new (similar) job within a reasonable period of time.

Differences between rescission and dismissal licence procedure

Differences between proceedings before the Cantonal Court and a dismissal licence procedure before the Regional Director and advantages of the former proceedings over the latter are:

(a) in the proceedings before the Cantonal Court there is an oral hearing of the case, which is decided by a professional judge;

(b) the Cantonal Court is not bound by the restrictions referred to above although the dismissal prohibitions may influence the Cantonal Court's decision; and

(c) the procedure before the Cantonal Court hardly ever takes more than eight weeks.

Breach of contract

Technically, an employment agreement may also be terminated through rescission by the Cantonal Court because of breach of contract. However, in practice this alternative is hardly ever chosen.

Mutual consent to have the agreement rescinded

To overcome the problem that the employee may forfeit his unemployment benefits if he agrees to termination of his employment, the parties often agree that the employee will not dispute the facts submitted by the employer in his petition for rescission and that the employer will pay the employee a certain compensation for the loss of his job.

This practice is, in general, accepted by the Cantonal Courts and the authorities for unemployment benefits.

2.7.4   EMPLOYMENT AGREEMENTS IN BANKRUPTCY

If the employer has been declared bankrupt, the appointed receiver and the employees may terminate the employment agreements, irrespective of whether they are for fixed terms or for indefinite periods of time. Notice periods must be observed. However, the employee is in any event entitled to terminate his employment agreement by giving six weeks' notice; under the new law this period is reduced to one month. The receiver in bankruptcy may in any event terminate employment agreements by giving six weeks' notice, but this notice period is extended by 13 weeks at the most in respect of employees who have reached the age of 45 but are younger than 65; under the new law it is simply stated that the receiver must observe the applicable statutory notice period. The dismissal prohibitions discussed above do not apply to termination by the receiver in bankruptcy. The possibility to request the Cantonal Court to dissolve the employment agreement remains available in bankruptcy. The receiver in bankruptcy does not have to obtain a dismissal licence from the Regional Director. However, the receiver in bankruptcy cannot terminate employment agreements without having been authorised to do so by the Supervisory Judge appointed in the bankruptcy (see also below section **8.4.3**). The provisions of the Act on notification of collective dismissals (see below) do not apply in bankruptcy.

A bankruptcy of the employee does not affect the employment agreement although the wages will have to be paid to the receiver.

2.7.5   THE ACT ON NOTIFICATION OF COLLECTIVE DISMISSALS

The Act on notification of collective dismissals provides that an employer who intends to terminate the employment of at least 20 of his employees working within the district of one of the Regional Labour Offices within a period of three months must notify the Regional Director and the 'interested trade unions'.

'Interested trade unions'
'Interested trade unions' are those trade unions which:
(a)   pursue the object of representing the interests of their members;
(b)   are active as such in the company or in the branch concerned; and
(c)   are known as such to the employer.

Collective bargaining agreements
Collective bargaining agreements often also contain provisions on providing information to and consultation with the trade unions in the event of reorganisations and collective dismissals.

Procedure
The employer can only validly dismiss the individual employees concerned after prior approval of the Regional Director.

The Regional Director will only consider a request for such approval after one month has lapsed after notification. Upon the coming into force of the bill referred to in section **2.1** the Act on notification of collective dismissals will also be changed. If the notification is accompanied by a statement from the relevant trade unions to the effect that they have been consulted, a request for approval is taken into consideration without delay. This period is extended to two months if the Regional Director finds out that one and the same employer has in any period of three months filed applications for dismissal of 20 or more employees without having made the said notification.

The request for approval of the Regional Director should set out the reasons for the proposed dismissals and, if not all employees employed by the employer will be dismissed, for the choice to dismiss the employees concerned (rather than others). The Regional Director will in principle apply the principle of seniority (the 'last in first out' rule). Exceptions to this rule can be made, eg if the preferred employee is better skilled or better qualified for the job in question than a more senior colleague. The reasons for such deviation from the seniority principle should be explained extensively to the Regional Director.

Proceedings with the Regional Director in cases of collective dismissals normally take two to three months after the individual requests have been submitted.

Social plan

Collective bargaining agreements often oblige the employer to agree on what is referred to as a 'social plan' which provides for severance payments. Also apart from the obligation on the basis of collective bargaining agreements, it is quite customary to agree with the trade unions on such a plan in the consultation with the trade unions. Normally, such social plans provide for income guarantees (by way of supplementary payments to the unemployment benefits received after termination or to the lower income which an employee may earn with another employer) for a period of time depending on such factors as age and length of service/employment.

However, irrespective of what has been discussed and/or agreed with the trade unions (and the works council), each individual employee is free to defend his or her own case, and is free to claim further damages on the ground that the dismissal is 'apparently unreasonable'.

2.8 COLLECTIVE BARGAINING AGREEMENTS

One of the main sources of Dutch employment law is formed by collective bargaining agreements (*collectieve arbeidso-vereenkomsten*; referred to as 'CAOs'). A collective bargaining agreement is an agreement between one or more employers or employers' associations and one or more trade unions in which rules are given for employment conditions which have to be observed in employment agreements.

The most important employers' associations are the Federation of Dutch Enterprises (VNO) which consists of various employers' organisations in trade, industry, transport, banking, insurance, wholesale and large retail stores, and the Dutch Christian Employers' Federation (NCW). There are also three agricultural organisations and an organisation for employers in small scale and retail businesses.

The most important trade unions in the Netherlands are the Federation of Dutch Trade Unions (FNV) and the National Federation of Christian Democratic Workers (CNV). There are separate smaller unions for high-ranking employees, which together form the Trade Unions Federation for Middle and Senior Staff Personnel (MHP).

The most important feature of a collective bargaining agreement is its so-called 'normative' effect. A collective bargaining agreement is binding upon an employer or an employee if the employer or employee is or becomes a member of an association or union which is a party to the collective bargaining agreement. A provision in a collective bargaining agreement on employment conditions which are intended to be applied to individual employment agreements is automatically (without further individual agreement) and as a mandatory provision (an individual agreement in deviation from it is void) applicable to an employment relationship between an employer and an employee who are both members of parties to the collective bargaining agreement. Collective bargaining agreements also have effect on employment agreements with employees who are not members of the union or unions which is or are party to the collective bargaining agreement. However, the normative provisions of the collective bargaining agreement are not automatically and by way of mandatory provisions part of the individual employment agreement with an 'unorganised' employee. Applicability of the normative provisions of the collective bargaining agreement requires a further individual agreement between the 'organised' employer and the 'unorganised' employee. In practice, however, an 'organised' employer will treat his employees equally irrespective of whether they are members of the trade union(s) which is (or are) party to the collective bargaining agreement.

General applicability

A collective bargaining agreement may be declared generally applicable. The Minister of Social Affairs and Employment may, at the request of one or more parties to a collective bargaining agreement, declare provisions from such agreement, which already apply to an important majority of employees working in one sector of industry, generally applicable for all employers and employees in that sector.

2.9 EMPLOYEES' SOCIAL SECURITY LAWS IN THE NETHERLANDS

The main social security laws for employees are:
(1) the Sickness Benefits Act (*Ziektewet*);
(2) the Act on Disability Insurance (*Wet op de arbeidsongeschikt-heidsverzekering*);
(3) the Unemployment Act (*Werkloosheidswet*); and
(4) the Health Insurance Act (*Ziekenfondswet*).

The protection of the minimum level of the benefits paid pursuant to the Acts referred to above (except the Health Insurance Act) is provided for in the Act on Additional Allowances (*Toeslagenwet*).

There is a separate Act on provision of income for elderly and partly disabled unemployed employees.

The Sickness Benefits Act, the Act on Disability Insurance and the Unemployment Act provide for a compulsory insurance of employees. Employees are defined as persons who are in private or public employment, which means they have a civil employment agreement as referred to in art 1637a of the Civil Code. The group of persons insured under these Acts is extended in the Acts themselves and in decrees based on the Acts. The extensions relate to groups of persons who do not fall within the definition of employees as referred to above.

3
MERGERS AND ACQUISITIONS

3.1 INTRODUCTION

A merger in the Netherlands can take place by:
(1) share purchase;
(2) purchase of business;
(3) 'legal' merger.

The first two types of merger are only briefly discussed in this paragraph. Legal merger will be described in more detail in section **3.2**.

Merger control in the Netherlands, in particular the provisions of the Merger Code, is discussed separately in section **3.3**.

The procedure for the 'squeezing out' of minority shareholders is described in section **3.4**.

Share purchase

As to the formalities of transferring registered shares, reference is made to section **1.3.2**. For the transfer of bearer shares, see section **1.3.4** and for the trade on the Amsterdam Stock Exchange, see section **5.3.4**.

When, as a result of a share purchase, a major holding in a listed company is acquired, disclosure must be made (see section **1.5.7**).

If a public offer on listed shares is made Chapter I of the Merger Code applies (see section **3.3.3**).

If a share purchase results in a 'merger', Chapter II of the Merger Code will apply (see section **3.3.4**).

The works councils in the companies involved may have a right of advice (see section **1.11.4**).

Purchase of business

The transfer of a business will involve more transfer formalities than a share purchase. Each asset or liability being part of the business will have to be transferred in accordance with the particular Dutch legal requirements regarding such asset or liability.

Employees of the enterprise (or part of it) which is being purchased will be protected by arts 1639aa–dd of the Civil Code providing for an automatic transition of the rights and obligations under existing employment agreements to the purchaser. The employees will automatically become employees of the purchaser (see further section **2.3**).

The rules of the Works Council Act and of Chapter II of the Merger Code must be observed.

3.2 'LEGAL' MERGER

General

The 'legal' merger was introduced in Dutch company law in 1984 to implement the third EC Company Law Directive of 9 October 1978 (Official Journal 1978 L295/36).

Legal merger is possible in respect of all Dutch legal entities but only Dutch legal entities. Only companies are dealt with in this paragraph.

In practice, the legal merger is not often used as a method to acquire a company. It is more commonly used within corporate groups as a method to simplify the group structure.

Different types of legal merger

In a legal merger there is always one 'acquiring' company and one or more 'disappearing' companies. A legal merger between companies may take place in various ways, including:

(1) company A merges into company B;
(2) company A and company B merge into a new company C;
(3) company A and B being 'sister' companies merge into existing parent company C.

In view of the scope of this book, these different types of mergers cannot be discussed in detail.

Consequences

As a result of a legal merger:

(1) the disappearing company(ies) cease to exist upon the merger taking effect;
(2) the shareholders of the disappearing company(ies) become

shareholders of the acquiring company, except in certain circumstances (see below);
(3) the acquiring company acquires all assets and liabilities of the disappearing company(ies) automatically by 'universal succession of title' (*verkrijging onder algemene titel*).

The shareholders of the disappearing company do not necessarily become shareholders of the acquiring company. Exceptions are:
(1) the shareholders of the disappearing company may receive *cash* instead of shares in the acquiring company but only to a total maximum of 10 per cent of the nominal value of the shares allotted to these shareholders;
(2) if a legal merger takes place between an 'acquiring' parent company and its 'disappearing' 100 per cent subsidiary, the shares in the subsidiary will be cancelled by operation of law;
(3) under certain circumstances, the shareholders of the disappearing company may receive shares in a group company (for instance, in the parent of the acquiring company).

Procedure

The procedure starts with a merger proposal drawn up jointly by the managing boards of the merging companies. This proposal must contain certain information, including the exchange ratio of the shares and the articles of association of the acquiring company as they will read after the merger. In addition, the managing board of each merging company must prepare a written statement setting out the reasons for the merger and its expected consequences. Furthermore, an expert (usually an accountant) must review the merger proposal and certify, *inter alia*, whether the proposed exchange ratio is reasonable.

The merger proposal, together with the expert's certificate and certain other documents, must be deposited at the offices of the companies and filed with the trade register. The filing is made public in a national newspaper.

The general meetings of shareholders of the merging companies *decide* on the merger, but not before one month after the filing has been made public. If the articles of association provide this, the managing board of the acquiring company may have the authority to decide on the merger.

The merger finally takes place by *notarial deed* and becomes effective on the date of the deed.

NB: The procedure for a merger between, *inter alia*, a parent and its 100 per cent subsidiary is much simpler.

Protection of interested parties

The creditors of the merging companies are protected in a similar way as in case of reduction of capital (see section **1.4.5**). Within one month after the filing of the merger proposal was made public, they may appeal to the District Court against the proposal to merge. The notarial deed for the merger may not be passed during this appeal.

The interests of other interested parties, such as the holders of a special right to distribution of profit, or a right of pledge in respect of shares in the disappearing company, are also protected.

3.3 MERGER CONTROL

3.3.1 INTRODUCTION

Merger control in the Netherlands has three aspects:

(1) *Monopoly law*: Apart from EC law on monopolies (which is not elaborated on in this chapter), no general monopoly rules exist in the Netherlands. There is no national 'monopoly' authority (such as in the UK) which must approve or receive notice of certain proposed mergers.

(2) *Rights of the works council*: The works councils—if any—in the companies which are parties to (or a target of) a merger will usually have the right to render advice on the proposed merger. The matters on which advice must be asked and the procedure are described in section **1.11.2**.

(3) *The Merger Code (Fusiegedragsregels)*: The Merger Code (see section **3.3.2**–section **3.3.4**) applies to public offers, and to all 'mergers' (this term includes take-overs) involving a company or a group of companies with more than 100 employees in the Netherlands.

NB: In the banking and insurance industry special rules for mergers and acquisitions apply (see for credit institutions section **4.1.2**).

3.3.2   THE MERGER CODE—GENERAL

The Merger Code is a set of rules of conduct first issued in 1970 by the Social and Economic Council (see **Introduction**) and amended in 1975 and 1990. The Code is designed to protect the interests of both shareholders and employees.

The Code does not have statutory effect. Failure to comply with its rules may lead to the Committee for Merger Affairs (see **Introduction**) imposing limited sanctions on the company(ies) involved. Such sanctions include a public notification of the company's non-compliance with the Merger Code. In practice, the business community in the Netherlands adheres quite strictly to the provisions of the Merger Code.

The Merger Code is divided into two chapters. Chapter I contains rules of conduct (for the protection of shareholders) to be observed in case of a public offer for shares. Chapter II contains rules of conduct (for the protection of employees) in case of a merger or take-over of an enterprise.

3.3.3   THE MERGER CODE—PUBLIC OFFER (CHAPTER I)

Scope

The rules of conduct in Chapter I of the Merger Code apply to:
(1)   a public offer for:
    (a)   shares, including depositary receipts of shares, in an NV which are listed, or regularly traded, in the Netherlands;
    (b)   securities which are listed, or regularly traded, in the Netherlands and which are convertible into shares in an NV;
(2)   a non-public offer for registered shares in an NV or BV if the offer is made to more than 50 per cent of the registered shareholders.

If a public offer is made for shares in a foreign company which are listed or regularly traded in the Netherlands, some publication and information provisions of Chapter I apply.

Types of public offer

A distinction is made between three types of public offers:

(1)   *Firm offer*: This is defined as a public offer to acquire shares in an NV, stating at least the price or exchange ratio offered.
(2)   *Partial offer*: This is a public offer to acquire a portion of the shares in an NV and stating at least the price or exchange ratio offered.
(3)   *Tender offer*: This is defined as an invitation to the public to tender their shares in an NV for a consideration to be determined by the holders of such shares themselves.

The rules of conduct

The rules make a distinction between friendly and hostile offers, ie offers with and offers without the agreement of the managing board of the target company.

The rules of conduct to be observed in case of a friendly offer are rather detailed. The following are the most essential:

(1)   A *public announcement* must be made in a friendly offer as soon as the negotiations between the managing boards of the offeror and the target company reach a stage which justifies the expectation that an agreement on the public offer can be reached.
(2)   If the public offer will lead to a 'merger' as defined in Chapter II of the Merger Code, the rules of conduct regarding information to and consultation with the trade unions will apply (see section **3.3.4**).
(3)   Within 30 days after the public announcement, the offeror must:
      (a)   make a public offer; or
      (b)   announce the decision not to make the offer; or
      (c)   indicate within which period a decision about the offer may be expected.
(4)   If a public offer is made, it must be announced in the Official Price List of the Amsterdam Stock Exchange (see section **5.3.2**) and/or in a national newspaper.
(5)   Within six weeks after a firm offer has been made, the offeror must make available a '*notice of offer*' (*aanbiedingsbericht*) setting out specific information about the offer.

       In case of a partial or tender offer, the announcement of the offer referred to in (4) must already contain information such as the percentage of shares which the offeror aims to acquire (NB: this percentage may not exceed 30 per cent).

(6)   The period of time during which the shares can be presented
      must be:
      (a)   at least seven days in case of a partial or tender offer;
            and
      (b)   at least 20 days in case of a public offer (30 days if the
            offer is hostile).
(7)   The managing and supervisory directors of both companies
      involved in the offer must comply with provisions to avoid
      insider dealing (see section **5.6**).
(8)   In case of a firm offer, a meeting of shareholders of the target
      company is convened at least eight days before the end of the
      presentation period. At this meeting the offer is discussed.
(9)   No later than five days after the end of the presentation
      period, the offeror must announce whether the offer will be
      honoured.

Hostile offer

If there is no agreement on the offer between the offeror and
the target company, the offeror must observe some additional
rules *before* a public announcement of the offer can be made.

These additional rules provide, *inter alia*, that the offeror
must first notify the managing board of the target company of its
intentions, inviting this managing board to discuss the offer with
him within seven days. In principle, the offeror must subsequently wait seven days before he makes his offer. The provision
is intended to avoid a 'raid' on the target company.

If the hostile offer is made to effect a 'merger' as defined in
Chapter II of the Merger Code, the managing board of the target
company must be notified at least 15 days before the offer is made.
This is to enable the consultation with the trade unions as
provided in Chapter II.

3.3.4   THE MERGER CODE—EMPLOYEE PROTECTION
(CHAPTER II)

Chapter II, which contains rules for the protection of
employees' interests in case of a 'merger' (see below), applies to:
(1)   a merger involving an enterprise established in the Nether-
      lands and regularly employing at least 100 employees; or
(2)   a merger involving an enterprise belonging to a group of

enterprises which employs at least 100 employees in the Netherlands.

An enterprise may be 'involved' as transferor, transferee or target company.

Exceptions

Chapter II does not apply to:

(1)   a merger of enterprises which are part of one group; or

(2)   to a merger which is outside the scope of Dutch law.

Exception (2) is explained by the Committee for Merger Affairs as follows. A merger of two foreign companies would not usually be considered to be within 'the scope of Dutch law', even if an enterprise held by one of these companies employs more than 100 employees in the Netherlands. However, if the merger transaction entered into abroad would only or mainly relate to the transfer of control in a Dutch enterprise, this would be considered within the scope of Dutch law.

Merger

A merger is defined as: 'any acquisition of direct or indirect control over the activities of an enterprise or part of it'.

Control of an enterprise may be acquired by a share purchase. If this purchase *results* in the holding of 50 per cent or more of the shares, this will usually be considered a 'merger'.

A 'merger' may also be effected by an asset purchase. If only a part of an enterprise is acquired, it will depend on the circumstances whether this constitutes a 'merger'. The Committee for Merger Affairs considers the acquisition of a branch and—under certain circumstances—the acquisition of a certain activity of the enterprise to be 'mergers'.

Demerger and joint venture

If a majority shareholding in a company is split up in two or more minority shareholdings, such a 'demerger' (*defusie*) would not be considered a 'merger' within the meaning of Chapter II. However, if this demerger is combined with a cooperation (joint venture) agreement between the shareholders, an 'acquisition of control' will be considered to have taken place by the joint venture partners jointly. Under such circumstances the rules of conduct must be observed.

Rules of conduct

The rules of conduct in Chapter II can be summarised as follows:

(1)   If a public announcement of a proposed merger is made, the trade unions concerned must be informed in advance of the contents of the announcement.

(2)   If merger negotiations reach 'a stage which justifies the expectation that agreement can be reached' the trade unions concerned must be notified of this at once. The same notification must be made to the Committee for Merger Affairs.

(3)   The trade unions must also be provided with information on:
   (a)   the reasons for the merger;
   (b)   the anticipated social, economic and legal consequences of the merger; and
   (c)   the proposed measures to be taken in connection with the merger.

   The information will be provided in writing unless the parties agree otherwise.

(4)   Subsequently, but before agreement on the merger is reached, a meeting will be held with the trade unions in which they can express their opinion. Several aspects of protection of employees' interests will be discussed, including for instance the moment of consultation with the works council on the proposed merger (see section **1.11.4**).

(5)   If the trade unions require further information to form an opinion, it must, if possible, be supplied to them.

(6)   The trade unions must keep the information referred to in (2) confidential unless they are released from this obligation.

   The information as referred to in (3), (4) and (5) must also be held confidential provided that the trade unions are informed by registered letter of this obligation.

   A trade union may state within four days of receiving this letter that it does not intend to keep the information confidential, but in such case the rules of conduct no longer have to be observed in respect of that trade union.

(7)   After agreement on merger has been reached, the Committee for Merger Affairs must be informed of the manner in which the rules of conduct have been applied.

   It follows from these rules of conduct that although

extensive consultation with the trade unions is required, *no consensus* needs to be reached on the proposed merger. The powers of the works council are in this respect more extensive than those of the trade unions, as they include the right to appeal against the decision to merge if this does not conform with the works council's advice.

Moment of 'justifiable expectation'

The moment on which 'the expectation that agreement will be reached is justified', ie the moment on which the trade unions have to be informed for the first time, is often difficult to determine.

In its explanatory comments on the Merger Code, the Committee for Merger Affairs has pointed out that it is essential that consultation with the trade unions takes place *before* agreement has been reached. The moment of 'justifiable expectation' has arrived, according to the Committee for Merger Affairs, when the discussions about the *terms* of the merger are still proceeding and the parties are not yet morally or legally bound to each other in respect of the terms of the merger but do expect to be bound at a later stage.

A *letter of intent* may sometimes be considered an 'agreement'. This would be the case if it contains the agreement of the parties on the principal terms of the merger and is not merely a statement of intent to conduct negotiations on such principal terms. If this is the case, the moment of 'justifiable expectation' lies *before* the signing of the letter of intent and accordingly the consultation must take place before the signing.

3.4 'SQUEEZE OUT' OF MINORITY SHAREHOLDERS

General

A shareholder who holds nearly all shares in an NV or BV may, for various reasons, wish to acquire 100 per cent of the share capital. The minority shareholders, however, may refuse to sell their shares or—particularly in case of bearer shares—may be impossible to trace.

Under Book 2 Civil Code, a 95 per cent shareholder may 'squeeze out' the minority shareholders by filing a claim against them for the transfer of their shares.

Procedure

A claim on the basis of these provisions is filed with the Enterprise Division of the Court of Appeal in Amsterdam (see **Introduction**) by:

(1) a shareholder holding at least 95 per cent of the issued shares in the company; or

(2) two or more shareholders belonging to the same 'group', which together hold at least 95 per cent of the issued shares.

The claim must be filed against *all* other shareholders by serving individual writs of summons. A special procedure for serving the writ of summons against shareholders who are unknown or whose addresses are unknown is available.

Grounds

The claimant only has to state that he holds 95 per cent or more of the issued shares. The Enterprise Division may reject the claim (against all defendants) if:

(1) a defendant will suffer serious material loss as a result of the transfer;

(2) a defendant is the holder of a priority share (see above section **1.3.1**); or

(3) the claimant has waived its right to make the claim *vis-à-vis* a defendant.

Price and transfer

The Enterprise Division determines the price of the shares on a date to be determined by it. If necessary an expert will report on the value of the shares first.

If the Enterprise Division decides in favour of the claimant, it will order the claimant to pay the price of the shares (plus interest accrued after the fixed date) and order the defendant(s) to transfer the shares to the claimant.

The claimant must notify the defendant(s) of the day and place of payment and the price of the shares.

The claimant may also use an alternative method of having the shares transferred if one or more defendants are unknown or unwilling to cooperate. In this method, the claimant pays the price of the shares (with interest accrued) into a special account designated by the Act on the Deposit of Monies (*Consignatiewet*). By payment into this account the claimant will acquire the unencumbered right to the shares concerned.

4
BANKING SUPERVISION AND EXCHANGE CONTROL

4.1 BANKING SUPERVISION IN THE NETHERLANDS

4.1.1 INTRODUCTION

General

Banking supervision in the Netherlands is based on the Act on the supervision of the credit system of 13 April 1978 (as amended) (*Wet toezicht kredietwezen*).

The following institutions are subject to supervision exercised by the Dutch Central Bank (*De Nederlandsche Bank*; referred to as 'DNB'):

(1) credit institutions;
(2) capital market institutions.

The exercise of supervision is one of the tasks imposed upon DNB by the Bank Act 1948.

Second EC Banking Directive

The Second Banking Directive of 15 December 1989 (as amended; Official Journal of 30 December 1989 L386/1) will render it necessary to amend the Act on the Supervision of the Credit System. At the time of writing a proposal is in the process of being prepared. It is expected that the amendments to the Act may be fairly substantial.

4.1.2 CREDIT INSTITUTIONS

Definition

Credit institutions are defined as 'legal entities, partnerships (*vennootschappen onder firma*), limited partnerships (*commanditaire vennootschappen*) which, and natural persons who, make it their business to obtain the disposal of funds, withdrawable daily or at less than two years' notice, whether or not in the form of savings, and to grant credits and make investments on their own account'.

Foreign enterprises and institutions acting as credit institutions in the Netherlands

The provisions of the Act apply to enterprises and institutions which are established outside the Netherlands and which engage in the business of credit institutions in the Netherlands through one or more offices, branches, agencies or permanent representatives. However, the provisions of the Act only apply to the business which such enterprises and institutions carry on in the Netherlands. DNB may stipulate that all or certain legal relationships between such foreign entities and natural persons or legal entities in the Netherlands are part of the business in the Netherlands and are therefore subject to supervision.

Licence and licence requirements

An enterprise or institution is only permitted to engage in the business of a credit institution after it has obtained a licence to do so from DNB. To obtain a licence the enterprise or institution must meet certain requirements:

(1)   the day to day policy must be determined by at least two persons who have sufficient experience in banking;

(2)   a credit institution in the form of a public limited liability company (*naamloze vennootschap*) or of a private limited liability company (*besloten vennootschap*) must have at least three supervisory directors (see Chapter 1);

(3)   the amount of the equity must at least be equal to the amount specified in a royal decree; at present, this amount is Dfl5m.

Register

After the licence has been granted, the credit institution is entered in a register which is open for inspection by the public.

Monetary supervision and 'prudential control'

Credit institutions are subject to monetary supervision and supervision in respect of solvency and liquidity (generally referred to as 'prudential control').

The activities of credit institutions are closely monitored by DNB and detailed reporting requirements must be complied with.

Statement of no-objection for certain actions

Credit institutions are not allowed, unless they have obtained a statement of no-objection:

(1) to reduce their equity by repayment of capital or distribution of reserves;

(2) to acquire, directly or indirectly, participations in other enterprises or institutions (participation meaning an interest exceeding 5 per cent of the equity of the enterprise or institution concerned or the exercise of a degree of control in the enterprise or institution concerned which is comparable to such interest) or to increase such participations;

(3) to take over the whole or a considerable part of the assets and liabilities of other enterprises or institutions;

(4) to merge with other enterprises or institutions;

(5) to proceed to a financial reorganisation; or

(6) to have a managing partner join the credit institution.

If a person can cast, or cause to be cast on his behalf, more than one-twentieth of the number of votes in the general meeting of shareholders or the meeting of partners of a credit institution, or is otherwise able to exercise, or cause to be exercised on his behalf, a comparable degree of direct or indirect control in a credit institution, such person will not be allowed to cast or cause to be cast such votes or to exercise or cause to be exercised such control until a statement of no-objection has been obtained.

An application for a statement of no-objection must be submitted to DNB. The statement of no-objection will be issued by the Minister of Finance.

4.1.3 'NEAR BANKS'

There used to be supervision of a category of financial institutions which were referred to as 'near banks'. They were legal entities, partnerships, limited partnerships which, and natural persons who, not being credit institutions, have obtained short-term funds (ie withdrawable within two years) in the amount of at least Dfl50m (or the equivalent in a foreign currency):

(1) from enterprises and institutions established in the Netherlands *other than* credit institutions; or

(2) by issuing debt securities denominated in Dutch guilders; or

(3) by a combination of (1) and (2).

They were obliged to notify DNB of such borrowing by registered letter and were subject to a certain (light) degree of monetary supervision. 'Near banks' had to report their cumulative outstanding short-term debts to DNB. Certain exemptions did, however, exist.

Supervision of 'near banks' was abolished when DNB announced in its circular letter of 27 September 1991 (see section **4.1.6** below) that the reporting requirement is no longer operative.

4.1.4 CAPITAL MARKET INSTITUTIONS

What are 'capital market institutions'?

The term 'capital market institutions' is not used in the Act on the supervision of the credit system. On the basis of the Act a royal decree (generally referred to as the 'Decree on supervision of other capital market institutions') has been issued which applies to legal entities, partnerships, limited partnerships which, and natural persons who, make it their business to obtain the disposal of funds from the public withdrawable at two years' notice or more and to grant credits on their own account, with the exception of:

(1) credit institutions;

(2) mortgage banks as referred to in art 1 of the Decree on supervision of mortgage banks;

(3) enterprises and institutions listed in art 2, para 2 of the First EC Council Directive of 12 December 1977 on the coordination of laws, regulations and administrative provisions relating to the taking up and pursuit of the business of credit institutions (Official Journal of the European Communities L322/30), whose creditors' interests are, in the opinion of the Minister of Finance, sufficiently safeguarded in another manner.

Source of the funds

It is important to note that there is no supervision in respect of borrowing long-term funds from professional providers of funds (ie non-public). Whether or not the funds are obtained from the public is, however, irrelevant in respect of credit institutions.

Application of funds

Other than the definition of credit institutions, the relevant royal decree on the supervision of capital market institutions does not refer to the making of investments by the institutions.

Licence and licence requirements

It is only permitted to carry on the business of a capital market institution after having obtained a licence. The requirements which have to be met to obtain such licence are substantially the same as those in respect of credit institutions.

Register

Capital market institutions are also entered in a register which is open for inspection by the public.

'Prudential control'

The supervision exercised by DNB in respect of capital market institutions is, however, limited to supervision relating to the institutions' solvency and liquidity.

Foreign enterprises and institutions acting as capital market institutions in the Netherlands

The relevant provisions of the Act on the supervision of the credit system and the royal decree based on the Act also apply to enterprises and institutions established outside the Netherlands which engage in the business of capital market institutions in the Netherlands through offices, branches, agencies or permanent representatives. Supervision is only exercised in respect of the business carried out in the Netherlands.

4.1.5 SANCTIONS

Criminal sanction

Violation of the statutory prohibitions, that is to be active as a credit or capital market institution without a licence, is an economic offence under the Economic Offences Act (*Wet Economische Delicten*).

Article 47 of the Act

Article 47 of the Act on the supervision of the credit system further provides that provisions in internal rules of or in agreements concluded by credit institutions which contravene the Act shall not apply. Article 47 of the Act also applies to capital market institutions. This article is expected to be repealed when a revised Act (see section **4.1.1**) comes into force.

General civil law consequences

Furthermore, under general principles of Dutch contract law an agreement, the due performance of which would result in a breach of statutory law, may be considered by Dutch courts to be null and void. This may also apply to debt instruments issued by enterprises or institutions which would have required a licence to do so. This does not necessarily mean, however, that the holders of the debt instruments can never obtain compensation from the issuer of such debt instruments.

4.1.6 DNB'S EXEMPTION POLICY FOR GROUP FINANCE COMPANIES

Dutch finance vehicles

Over the past few years a large number of foreign based groups of companies have set up Dutch companies (usually in the form of private limited liability companies (*besloten vennootschappen*)) as finance vehicles. The relatively mild tax climate for companies in the Netherlands has always been and still is an important reason for setting up a Dutch company through which funds can be raised for the group of companies to which it belongs.

General

As the funds are raised through short-term or long-term borrowing transactions and lent on to the other companies within the group which could be considered third parties, the activities of finance vehicles, technically speaking, fall within the scope of the Act on the supervision of the credit system. Depending on the type of borrowing transactions, a finance company can in fact be considered a credit institution or capital market institution. However, DNB has recognised that group financing activities were not meant to fall within the scope of the Act on the supervision of the credit system. From an economic point of view the on-lending of funds to group companies cannot be considered as granting credits to third parties which would constitute the business of a commercial bank.

Exemption policy

DNB has developed a policy to exempt group finance companies from the prohibitions of the Act on the supervision of the credit system. In this policy the group of companies as a whole, which uses a Dutch finance vehicle for fund raising, is itself considered as the borrowing entity. It is clear that the group of companies as such does not engage in the business of granting credits to third parties or making investments other than in its normal course of business.

Conditions

However, to be able to profit from this exemption policy, certain conditions need to be met. These conditions were originally set out in DNB's circular letter of 11 May 1990.

The proceeds of fund raising activities had to be kept within the group of companies to which the finance vehicle belongs. The obligations of the finance vehicle had to be guaranteed by its parent company. Deviations from these requirements were in certain circumstances accepted.

Especially in the year following the issue of the May 1990 circular letter it became increasingly clear that a large number of finance companies do not wish to confine their activities to traditional group financing. As going beyond group financing (eg by investing in securities issued by non-group companies) meant that the finance companies risked being considered as credit or capital market institutions, extensive discussions about the problems that had arisen between DNB and various parties involved took place in 1991. The discussions resulted in the issue of new policy guidelines in DNB's circular letter of 27 September 1991. In broad terms, the new guidelines have made it much easier for finance companies to apply funds raised by them to purposes other than group financing, without being considered as credit or capital market institutions.

Activities outside the scope of the Act

Finance companies which fund themselves exclusively by obtaining:
(1)   funds from within the group; and/or
(2)   *long-term* funds (ie with a maturity of two years or more) from professional market parties such as banks, insurance companies and pension funds,

do not fall within the definition of credit or capital market institutions at all.

Provided that these finance companies do not engage in attracting any other funds, they are free to use the funds as they like. DNB's guidelines do not affect them.

Group financing

A finance company which places at least 95 per cent of its 'balance sheet total' within the group will not be considered a credit or capital market institution by DNB. The source of the finance companies' funds is in that case irrelevant.

As under the old policy, the parent company must give a guarantee or enter into a keep well agreement. Other forms of security may be accepted by DNB.

On-lending or investing outside the group

Under the new guidelines a finance company may on-lend or invest funds outside the group if certain conditions are met:

(1) The first condition relates to the *source* of the funds. The funds must have been provided *exclusively* by:

    (a) the professional market parties (listed in Appendix A to the new guidelines and consisting of *inter alia* banks and institutional investors); alone or together with

    (b) group companies.

(2) The second condition relates to the *use* of the funds. The funds may *only* be:

    (a) on-lent to or invested in the parties described in the same Appendix A to the new guidelines; and/or

    (b) invested in securities which are:

        (i) listed on officially recognised stock exchanges in the EC or the G–10 countries and/or are registered with the United States Securities and Exchange Commission; or

        (ii) listed on other sufficiently regulated stock exchanges approved by DNB.

As in the case of group financing, a guarantee or keep well agreement or similar security must be provided. In addition, if the finance company obtains the funds from the abovementioned 'professionals' by issuing debt instruments *to bearer* which have a denomination of less than Dfl1m or the equivalent in another currency, a selling restriction must be imposed (Appendix B to the new guidelines).

Mixed activities

A finance company which takes funds from the *public*, in addition to funds from professional market parties, does not fall outside the scope of the Act on the supervision of the credit system and cannot profit from the provisions described in the preceding paragraph. It will have to comply fully with the group financing requirements. Therefore, it may only invest or on-lend up to 5 per cent of its balance sheet total outside the group. In other words, one finance company cannot 'mix' public and non-public funds and at the same time lend or invest more than 5 per cent of its total funds outside the group.

Transition period

The new guidelines will apply immediately to all activities undertaken by Dutch finance companies after 27 September 1991. Those finance companies whose activities on 27 September 1991 were not in compliance with the new guidelines, were given the opportunity to restructure their existing activities (without new breaches of the guidelines) before 1 January 1993.

4.1.7   ARTICLE 42 OF THE ACT ON THE SUPERVISION OF THE CREDIT SYSTEM

General rule

Another important provision of the Act on the supervision of the credit system is art 42. Article 42, para 1, substantially provides that it is prohibited to approach the public or to act as intermediary in any way for the purpose of commercially soliciting funds below a sum specified by the Minister of Finance. At present this sum is Dfl 100,000.

Credit institutions and capital market institutions which have obtained the required licence to carry on their business are not caught by this prohibition.

Exemptions

(1)   According to para 2 of art 42 the Minister of Finance may grant exemption or, on request, dispensation from the prohibition of the first paragraph. Such exemption or dispensation may be made subject to certain conditions.

(2) In a royal decree the Minister of Finance has set out general exemptions from the prohibition of art 42, para 1. Exempt from the prohibition is the raising of funds against the issue of documents of value to bearer, such as stamps or the like, as part of a sales transaction in wholesale, industrial or retail trading. More important is the exemption for the raising of funds against the issue of securities for which admission to the official listing on a supervised stock exchange in one of the EC Member States has been obtained or will be obtained.

However, the issue of debt securities with a denomination of at least Dfl 100,000 (or the equivalent of this amount in a foreign currency) escapes the prohibition of para 1 of art 42 altogether, even if the debt securities have not been and will not be officially listed on a stock exchange in an EC Member State.

Criminal sanction

Violation of the prohibition of para 1 of art 42 is also an economic offence under the Economic Offences Act.

4.2 EXCHANGE CONTROL

No exchange control

Since the deregulation of the capital markets in the Netherlands in January 1986 non-residents have acquired considerable freedom to borrow monies on these markets. With a view to this development, the last exchange control measures were abolished on 1 October 1986 (Statement of DNB of 11 September 1986).

Centralisation of payments; administrative regulations

At the same time new implementation regulations on the centralisation of payments to and from foreign countries and on general permits for such payments came into force. DNB also issued new General Administrative Regulations relating to the supply of information and details to DNB. These regulations do not impose restrictions but have as their object to ensure complete reporting to DNB for a correct composition of the balance of payments and for the support of the financial and monetary policy. The obligations undertaken by the Netherlands in international organisations (IMF, OECD and EC) have further limited the scope for a system of exchange controls.

Act on financial relations with foreign countries
The regulations are based on the Act on financial relations with foreign countries (*Wet financiële betrekkingen buitenland*). The principle of this Act is freedom to carry out financial transactions which involve foreign countries. The consequences of this principle are:
(1)   if there are no regulations prohibiting a certain transaction, it will be permitted;
(2)   the categories of payments in respect of which regulations may be issued, are explicitly set out in the Act;
(3)   the intervention of the authorities responsible for monetary affairs (the Minister of Finance and the Dutch Central Bank) is also, as far as the movement of capital is concerned, based on objectives which are explicitly set out for 'normal' as well as 'abnormal' circumstances.

Powers of DNB
On the basis of the Act DNB may, with the consent of the Minister of Finance, issue regulations which oblige residents of the Netherlands to make and receive payments to and from non-residents through the intermediary of financial institutions authorised by DNB. Such regulations have been issued by way of the implementation regulations referred to above.

To prevent disturbances of the Dutch capital markets resulting from financial relations with foreign countries, DNB may, again with the consent of the Minister of Finance, also issue regulations with respect to the following acts by residents or certain groups of residents:
(1)   to cooperate in the public or private placement of foreign securities;
(2)   to introduce foreign securities on a Dutch stock exchange;
(3)   to provide loans and credit facilities to non-residents to the extent they exceed the set amount and time period and to the extent they do not directly relate to transactions for the supply of goods or services;
(4)   to obtain foreign bonds denominated in Dutch guilders or in Dutch guilders and another currency or to obtain other similar securities whereby the amount of principal or

interest or both is or are linked to the exchange rate of the Dutch guilder against another currency;

(5)   to acquire shares or participations in investment institutions established abroad;

(6)   the borrowing of monies by way of a private or a public loan by finance companies established in the Netherlands to the extent that the monies borrowed are directly or indirectly for the purpose of financing foreign based companies and to the extent that the relevant transaction exceeds the amount determined by DNB.

The regulations relating to (some of) the Acts listed above, which had been issued by DNB in 1981, were abolished in 1986. Since then, DNB has not used its authority under the Act to give rules on those subjects.

Outflow and influx of capital

The Act on financial relations with foreign countries further enables the Minister of Finance to take measures if:

(1)   a large outflow of capital causes a considerable decrease of the reserves position of the Netherlands or if such development is threatening to occur; or if

(2)   a large influx of capital to a considerable extent frustrates the financial and economic policy in the Netherlands or if such development is threatening to occur.

The measures taken by the Minister of Finance may relate to:

(1)   the maintenance of bank accounts abroad or of foreign currency bank accounts in the Netherlands by residents of the Netherlands and the maintenance of bank accounts in the Netherlands by non-residents;

(2)   transactions in foreign currencies to which a resident of the Netherlands is a party;

(3)   the granting of loans and credits and the making of advance payments by residents to non-residents and *vice versa*;

(4)   transactions in securities and gold between residents and non-residents;

(5)   the provision of guarantees and other security interests to non-residents;

(6)   other acts of residents in connection with outflow of capital from or influx of capital into the Netherlands.

Supply of information to DNB

Article 13 of the Act contains the important provision that every person is obliged to supply information and details to DNB which are relevant to the composition of the balance of payments and to the determination and implementation of the measures which—pursuant to various provisions of the Act—may be taken by DNB and the Minister of Finance.

The supply of information and details must take place in accordance with the rules and regulations issued by DNB. These are the General Administrative Regulations relating to the supply of information and details to the Dutch Central Bank as referred to above.

There are regulations on information to be provided by residents to authorised financial institutions through which payments are made by residents to non-residents and *vice versa*. Residents must report the maintenance of bank accounts with foreign banks or other financial institutions. They must also provide details on transactions with non-residents which are effected in a manner other than through the intermediary of authorised financial institutions or via accounts held abroad, such as direct capital investments and compensation arrange- ments. The following residents must register with DNB (Department Balance of Payments):

(1)   residents who or which receive funds from non-residents with respect to goods which have not been or will not be brought into the free trade in the Netherlands;

(2)   residents who or which carry on foreign exchange bureaus;

(3)   resident enterprises and institutions (no matter what legal form they have) in which non-residents participate, directly or indirectly through share capital or otherwise, and which have as their object, or to a considerable extent engage in, obtaining funds from non-residents and the onward pay- ment of such funds to non-residents; group finance vehicles (see section **4.1.6**) will generally qualify as such and will therefore have to be registered as so-called 'special financial institutions';

(4)   residents who or which, whether or not for consideration, obtain funds from non-residents for onward payment to other non-residents; and

(5)   other residents to be determined by DNB.

Violation of the rules and regulations of or issued pursuant to the Act on financial relations with foreign countries is an economic offence under the Economic Offences Act.

4.3 DNB'S POLICY FOR THE ISSUE OF DEBT SECURITIES TO BEARER DENOMINATED IN DUTCH GUILDERS

Present guidelines

DNB has issued various guidelines to be observed upon the issue of debt securities to bearer denominated in Dutch guilders. The guidelines as presently in force can be summarised as follows:

(1)   Guilder debt securities to bearer indicated as 'long-term' must have a stated maturity of two years or longer.

(2)   Guilder debt securities to bearer indicated as 'short-term' ('commercial paper' issued by enterprises and institutions other than credit institutions and medium-term notes in Guilders and 'certificates of deposit' issued by credit institutions) must preferably have a minimum denomination of Dfl 1m.

(3)   The lead manager or lead managers of the bank syndicate which arranges the issue of the Guilder debt securities must comply with certain notification requirements; 'calendar procedures' apply to:

(a)   the issue of long-term bearer paper in the amount of Dfl 50m or more;

(b)   the issue of short-term bearer paper irrespective of volume;

(c)   programmes for the continuous issue of short-term bearer paper (Guilder 'commercial paper' on 'certificates of deposit' programmes); and

(d)   programmes for the continuing issue of medium-term bearer paper.

(4)   The lead manager of issues of bearer paper or of programmes under which such paper will be issued on an ongoing basis must meet certain requirements. The most important requirement is that the lead manager (which may be a Dutch subsidiary of a foreign financial institution) must be registered as a credit institution in the Netherlands under the Act on the supervision of the credit system.

5

SECURITIES AND EXCHANGE BUSINESS

5.1 SUPERVISION OF THE SECURITIES TRADE

5.1.1 INTRODUCTION

Supervision of the securities trade in order to enhance the adequate operation of the securities markets and to protect the interests of investors is necessary to preserve the good reputation of the Netherlands as one of the financial centres in Europe.

At the time of writing it was expected that the Act on the supervision of the securities trade of 7 March 1991 (*Wet toezicht effectenverkeer*) (the 'ASST') would come into force in June 1992. The ASST replaces the Exchange Act 1914 (*Beurswet 1914*) and the Securities Act (*Wet effectenhandel*). Together with the Act on the supervision of investment institutions (the 'ASII') the ASST provides a comprehensive system of supervision necessary to achieve the objects referred to above.

5.1.2 CONTENTS OF THE ASST

The ASST deals with the following subjects:
(1) the prospectus for the offering of securities;
(2) the periodical supply of relevant financial information with respect to securities;
(3) the profession or trade of intermediary in securities transactions (*effectenbemiddelaar*) or fund manager (*vermogensbeheerder*);
(4) the supervision of (stock) exchanges; and
(5) exchange of information with foreign authorities on the actual supervision of the securities trade.

5.1.3 KEY PROVISIONS OF THE ASST

First prohibition
It is illegal to offer securities upon issue or to hold out the

prospect of such an offer by means of advertisements or documents in or from within the Netherlands and outside a 'closed circle' or limited group.

Definition of securities
    The definition of securities in the ASST includes share certificates, debentures, option certificates, warrants, participation rights (*rechten van deelneming*), futures and depositary receipts of all such securities.

'Closed Circle'
    The explanatory memorandum to the ASST sets out the criteria to be applied in determining whether there is a 'closed circle'. The group of persons to which securities are offered will be considered a 'closed circle' if:
(1)   the number of persons is small and the group is precisely described or defined;
(2)   the persons in the group have a certain relationship with the offeror, which implies that apart from the financial relationship between the parties involved there must be other relationships; and
(3)   it has been made clear that acceptance of the offer is exclusively open to the group of persons which meets the two conditions referred to above.

Exceptions
    The prohibition to offer securities upon issue outside a 'closed circle' does not apply if:
(1)   the securities (to be) offered have been or will most likely shortly be admitted for listing on a recognised stock exchange in the Netherlands; or
(2)   if there is an offer, a prospectus meeting certain requirements (set out in a royal decree based on the ASST) is available and this prospectus is referred to in each written announcement of the offer; or
(3)   in case of the prospect of an offer being held out, certain requirements (also set out in a royal decree based on the ASST) are met in respect of such activity; or
(4)   the securities (to be) offered are participation rights (*rechten van deelneming*) of an investment institution registered pursuant to the ASSI (see section **5.2**); or

(5) an exemption or dispensation from the prohibition has been granted by the Minister of Finance.

General exemption

In an exemption regulation based on the ASST a general exemption from the prohibition will—*inter alia*—be granted in respect of the offering of securities to 'professional' parties such as insurance companies, pension funds, brokers and others who trade or invest in securities in the course of their profession or trade. It is also expected that the offering of securities exclusively to persons outside the Netherlands will be exempt.

Providing of information

Institutions securities of which have been issued outside a 'closed circle' and have not been admitted for listing on a recognised stock exchange, must periodically provide information on their financial position and must disclose facts which could have a material effect on the price of the relevant securities. The information and the manner in which it is made available must meet certain requirements set out in a royal decree based on the ASST. Exemption or dispensation from this obligation may be granted.

For listed institutions the obligation to provide relevant financial information is set out in the 'Rules relating to the requirements for listing on the Official Market of the ASE' (*Fondsenreglement*; there are similar rules for the Parallel Market; see section **5.3.2**).

Second prohibition

The second prohibition contained in the ASST is to (offer to) render services, without a licence, to natural persons or legal entities who or which do not belong to a 'closed circle' or limited group in or from within the Netherlands as an intermediary in securities transactions (*effectenbemiddelaar*).

Definition of intermediary

An intermediary in securities transactions (*effectenbemiddelaar*) is defined as:

(1) a person—this includes a legal entity—who, in carrying on

the profession or trade of intermediary and not being a fund manager (see below) is involved in the conclusion of securities transactions;

(2)   a person who, in the course of his profession or trade, offers the possibility to open a securities account, by means of which securities transactions may be concluded;

(3)   a person who, in his capacity of dealer in securities, carries out securities transactions for his own account in order to maintain a market in securities or gain a profit from a difference between asking prices and offering prices of securities (this is what is generally known as 'market making').

Licence

To be able to carry on business as an intermediary in securities transactions a licence is required. The Minister of Finance will grant such licence if certain requirements are met. The requirements relate to:

(1)   expertise and trustworthiness;

(2)   financial resources;

(3)   business management;

(4)   information to be made available to the public.

The requirements are further elaborated in a royal decree based on the ASST. A licence may be made subject to certain restrictions. The restrictions may only relate to the extent of the licence and the time period for which it is granted.

Exemptions

Intermediaries in securities transactions who are members of an exchange recognised under the Act (Amsterdam Stock Exchange, European Options Exchange and Financial Futures Market Amsterdam, see below section 5.3–section 5.5) are exempt from the prohibition to the extent that their intermediary activities relate to securities which have been admitted for listing on that stock exchange or which most likely will shortly be admitted for such listing. These exempt intermediaries must comply with the rules of the relevant stock exchange.

In an exemption regulation based on the ASST a general exemption will also be granted to—*inter alia*—intermediaries who are members of an official stock exchange in another EC

Member State. This exemption will also be limited to activities related to securities (likely to be) admitted for listing on the relevant exchange.

Those intermediaries who offer their services exclusively to 'professional parties' are also expected to be included in the list of exempted intermediaries in the exemption regulation.

Third prohibition

The same prohibition and the same exemptions which apply to intermediaries in securities transactions also apply to fund managers (*vermogensbeheerders*).

Definition of fund manager

A 'fund manager' is defined as a person who, in the course of his profession or trade and on the basis of an agreement, administers securities, belonging to a natural person or legal entity or administers monies for investment in securities, including the conclusion of securities transactions—or causing such securities transactions to be concluded—for the account of the person who is party to the agreement.

Register

There is a register in which the intermediaries in securities transactions and property administrators who are allowed to carry on their business pursuant to a licence or an exemption, are entered. The register is open for inspection by the public.

Fourth prohibition

The fourth prohibition contained in the ASST is to carry on a stock exchange without having obtained recognition from the Minister of Finance. The Amsterdam Stock Exchange, the European Options Exchange and the Financial Futures Market Amsterdam are recognised stock exchanges within the meaning of the ASST.

Implementation of EC rules and regulations

The Minister of Finance has the power to give directions to organisations, the members of which have admission to a recognised stock exchange and to entities carrying on stock exchanges in order to implement EC directives on the securities trade.

Powers of Minister of Finance

The Minister of Finance has far-reaching powers to investigate whether the provisions of the ASST and the rules and regulations based on it are complied with. The Minister of Finance may also exercise his powers under this Act to determine whether there is any reason to report insider dealing (see section **5.6**).

Securities Board

Part of the tasks and powers of the Minister of Finance on the basis of the ASST have been delegated to the Securities Board (*Stichting Toezicht Effectenverkeer*). The Securities Board is a foundation which was established on 21 July 1988 by the Stock Exchange Association and the Association European Options Exchange. The supervision of the Amsterdam Stock Exchange, the European Options Exchange and the Financial Futures Market in Amsterdam had already been delegated to the Securities Board on 1 February 1989. On the basis of the ASST, the Securities Board will now also have tasks and powers with respect to the securities trade which takes place off the exchanges.

5.1.4 THE PRINCIPLE OF RECIPROCITY

According to a special provision of the ASST a licence may be refused or withdrawn, a licence may be made subject to limitations or provisions or such limitations or provisions may be amended if:

(1) the intermediary in securities transactions or fund manager is established in a country which is not an EC Member State where Dutch financial institutions are not admitted or where they are made subject to unreasonable limitations; or if

(2) a natural person or legal entity with nationality of the country referred to above can directly or indirectly exercise a substantial power in the business of the intermediary or fund manager.

5.1.5 SANCTIONS

Violation of various provisions of the ASST or of provisions in regulations based on the ASST constitutes a criminal offence under the Economic Offences Act.

A dispensation or a licence may also be withdrawn, but only in a limited number of circumstances specifically described in the ASST.

5.1.6 APPEAL

Decisions on admission of securities for listing on the markets of recognised exchanges are taken by the organisers of such exchanges. These decisions may be appealed from with the Minister of Finance or—after delegation—the Securities Board.

Persons whose interests are affected by decisions taken by the Minister of Finance or the Securities Board on the basis of the ASST may appeal from such decisions with the Court of Appeal for Trade and Industry (*College van Beroep voor het bedrijfsleven*).

5.2 SUPERVISION OF INVESTMENT INSTITUTIONS

5.2.1 INTRODUCTION

On 15 October 1990 the Act on the supervision of investment institutions (*Wet toezicht beleggingsinstellingen*) ('ASII') came into force.

The ASII envisages to provide comprehensive rules relating to investment institutions with a view to an adequate operation of the financial markets and the protection of investors on such markets.

The ASII replaces a previous proposal for legislation on investment institutions as well as the provisions in the old Securities Act with regard to (mutual) investment funds.

It also forms the implementation of the EC Directive of 20 December 1985 relating to undertakings for collective investment in transferable securities, 'UCITS' (85/611/EEC; Official Journal of the European Communities L 375).

Together with the Act on the supervision of the securities trade ('ASST') (see section **5.1**), the ASII provides a comprehensive regulation of the exchange and securities business.

5.2.2 KEY PROVISIONS OF THE ASII

Prohibition

It is prohibited to solicit or to obtain monies or other goods in order to participate in an investment institution (*beleggingsin-*

stelling) which has not been granted a licence, or to offer rights of participation (*rechten van deelneming*) in such an investment institution.

Definition of investment institution

An investment institution is:

(1)   an investment company (*beleggingsmaatschappij*), ie a legal entity which solicits or has obtained monies or other goods for collective investment in order to allow the participants to share in the proceeds of the investments; or

(2)   an investment fund or unit trust (*beleggingsfonds*), ie property not constituting a separate legal entity and consisting of monies or other goods which have been solicited or obtained for collective investment, in order to allow the participants to share in the proceeds of the investments.

'Closed circle'

The prohibition only applies if these activities are carried out in or from within the Netherlands and outside a 'closed circle' or limited group. The activities are only considered to be carried out within a 'closed circle' or limited group and therefore escape the prohibition if:

(1)   the activities are addressed to a small number of persons;

(2)   there is not just a financial relationship between the institution and the persons to whom the institution addresses its activities;

(3)   it is made clear by the institution that acceptance of its offer is limited to the group of persons concerned.

These are the same criteria as apply in respect of the term 'closed circle' in the ASST (see section **5.1.3**).

Exceptions

The prohibition does not apply to an investment institution which has its seat (or of which the manager has its seat) in another EC Member State—provided that this Member State has implemented the EC Directive referred to above in section **5.2.1**—which has, as its exclusive object, to invest in securities with application of the principle of spreading of risk and the participation rights of which are—directly or indirectly—repurchased or redeemed at the request of the participants. A

'UCIT' from another EC Member State does, however, have an information obligation and is subject to a two months' waiting period and certain other requirements (see below).

The prohibition also does not apply to the offering of participation rights by natural persons otherwise than in the course of their profession or trade.

Licence requirements

The Dutch Central Bank, to which the Minister of Finance has delegated most of his tasks and powers under the ASII, will, on request, grant a licence to an investment institution if certain requirements are met. These requirements are set out in detail in the Royal Decree on the supervision of investment institutions, which contains provisions implementing various rules of the ASII. The requirements relate to:

(1) expertise and trustworthiness;
(2) financial resources;
(3) business management; and
(4) information to be made available to the participants in the investment institution and to the public in general.

If a licence for an investment fund (not being a separate legal entity; see above) is applied for, the applicant must also show that:

(1) the manager of the fund is a legal entity;
(2) the assets of the investment fund are deposited with a custodian independent from the manager; and
(3) the assets of the investment fund are separated from the property of the manager, of the custodian and of any other natural person or legal entity.

Additional requirements apply to the investment institution (and the custodian if there is one):

(1) which has as its exclusive object the investment in securities on the basis of the principle of spreading of risk; and
(2) the participation rights of which are—directly or indirectly—repurchased or redeemed at the request of the participant; and therefore falls within the scope of the UCITS directive; and
(3) which has its seat—or, if it is an investment fund, of which the manager has its seat—in the Netherlands.

However, these additional requirements do not apply if the Dutch 'UCIT'—*inter alia*—does not solicit or obtain monies or other goods from the public in EC Member States or mainly invests its assets through subsidiary companies in other subjects for investment than securities as defined by the ASII.

Licence restrictions

A licence may be made subject to certain restrictions with a view to an adequate operation of the financial markets and the protection of investors on such markets, if certain facts and circumstances relating to the investment institution render this necessary.

Compliance with rules by licensed investment institutions

A licensed investment institution must comply with the rules set out in the Royal Decree on the supervision of investment institutions. Like the requirements which must be met to obtain a licence, the rules that have to be observed by licensed institutions relate to:
(1) expertise and trustworthiness;
(2) financial resources;
(3) business management; and
(4) information to be made available to the Minister of Finance or the entity to which the Minister of Finance has delegated (part of) his tasks and powers on the basis of the ASII.

A licensed Dutch 'UCIT', to which additional licence requirements apply as has been discussed above, may not amend its articles of association or its other regulations if the 'UCIT' would through such an amendment cease to comply with these requirements.

If a Dutch 'UCIT' intends to trade its rights of participation in another EC Member State, it must inform the Dutch Central Bank and the competent authority in the other EC Member State.

Exemption

In a regulation based on the ASII the Minister of Finance has granted a general exemption from the prohibition of the Act to— *inter alia*—investment institutions which address their activities exclusively to natural persons who, and/or legal entities which, trade or invest in securities in the course of their profession or trade. Examples of such 'professionals' are banks, brokers, insurance companies and pension funds.

'UCITS' from other EC Member States

As discussed above, investment institutions which have their seat in another EC Member State and which have as their exclusive object the investment in securities on the basis of the principle of spreading of risk and the participation rights of which are—directly or indirectly—repurchased or redeemed at the request of the participants, are not caught by the prohibition if the Member State where the seat is located has implemented the EC Directive.

Providing information

Nevertheless, such an investment institution is obliged to inform the Dutch Central Bank of its intention to offer participation rights in the Netherlands outside a 'closed circle'. It must produce various documents to the Dutch Central Bank such as its prospectus and—*inter alia*—provide details on the way in which it intends to inform its participants and the public in general and on the way in which it intends to trade, pay out on, repurchase or redeem its participation rights in the Netherlands.

Waiting period

After the 'UCIT' from another EC Member State has informed the Dutch Central Bank, there is a waiting period of two months. Upon expiry of that period it may start its business of trading its participation rights, unless the Dutch Central Bank has informed the investment institution that its intentions with regard to informing the public and the trading etc of its participation rights in the Netherlands are not in accordance with applicable provisions of Dutch law or that the intended way of trading is contrary to provisions of Dutch law relating to subjects outside the scope of the EC Directive.

Obligations

The 'UCIT' from another EC Member State is obliged to take the necessary steps in order to see to it that payments are made on participation rights in the Netherlands and that such participation rights are repurchased or redeemed. It must also see to it that the required information is made available.

The Dutch Central Bank may prohibit the investment institution from offering its participation rights in the Netherlands (or make such offering subject to certain restrictions) if the rules referred to above are not complied with.

Register

The Dutch Central Bank keeps a public register in which the following investment institutions are entered:

(1) those which have been granted a licence; the entry includes a reference to any restrictions to which the licence has been made subject;

(2) investment institutions from other EC Member States which are allowed to trade their participation rights;

(3) (mutual) investment funds which upon the coming into force of this Act already had a licence (or an exemption) under the old Securities Act.

Powers of the Dutch Central Bank

The Dutch Central Bank has extensive powers to check whether the provisions of the ASII and the rules and regulations promulgated pursuant to it are complied with. The Dutch Central Bank may request that certain information be made available and may start investigations with licence applicants, with investment institutions or their custodians and with organisations of investment institutions to which—because of their membership of such organisations—an exemption under the Act has been granted.

5.2.3   THE PRINCIPLE OF RECIPROCITY

The Minister of Finance may refuse or withdraw a licence or make the licence subject to certain restrictions or change restrictions which have previously been imposed if the invest- ment institution has its seat in a non-EC country where Dutch financial institutions are not admitted or where unreasonable restrictions are imposed on Dutch financial institutions. The Minister of Finance has the same powers if a natural person or legal entity which has such country's nationality can directly or indirectly exercise control in the investment institution.

5.2.4   SANCTIONS

Violation of various provisions of, or pursuant to, the ASII constitutes an economic offence under the Economic Offences Act.

In a limited number of circumstances specifically described in the Act a licence may be withdrawn.

5.2.5 APPEAL

Any person whose interests are directly affected by a decision taken on the basis of the Act by the Minister of Finance or the Dutch Central Bank may appeal against such a decision with the Court of Appeal for Trade and Industry (*College van Beroep voor het bedrijfsleven*).

5.3 THE AMSTERDAM STOCK EXCHANGE

5.3.1 INTRODUCTION

Stock Exchange Association

The only stock exchange in the Netherlands, the Amsterdam Stock Exchange (the 'ASE'), is organised by the Stock Exchange Association (*Vereniging voor de Effectenhandel*), a private association established in 1876 which, since 1973, can be considered as the national organisation for the trade in securities.

Other corporations

The Stock Exchange Association holds shares in a number of corporations which render services to their participants (and others) and which play an important part in the trading, clearing, custody and administration of securities (see section **5.3.4**). These corporations are:

(1) the Centre for the Administration of Securities BV (*Centrum voor Fondsenadministratie*);
(2) Securities Clearing BV (*Effectenclearing BV*);
(3) Netherlands Central Institute for Giro Securities Transactions BV (*Nederlands Centraal Instituut voor Giraal Effectenverkeer BV; Necigef*);
(4) Kas-Associatie NV; and
(5) Nominee Amsterdam Stock Exchange NV and ASAS Servicing Company NV.

Two markets

There are two markets and thus two types of listing of securities on the ASE:

(1)   the Offical Market (*Officiële Markt*); and
(2)   the Parallel Market (*Parallelmarkt*).
The Parallel Market was set up on 1 February 1982. It may be considered as a continuation of the unofficial market for unlisted securities which already existed before 1982.

Main difference
The main difference between the Official Market and the Parallel Market relates to the requirements for admission to listing. The requirements for listing on the Official Market are more stringent than those for listing on the Parallel Market. On the Official Market the application for listing must be made for all issued securities of a particular category (*fonds*, see below). This is not the case on the Parallel Market.

5.3.2   LISTING ON THE ASE

Listing requirements
The rules relating to the requirements for listing on the Official Market of the ASE (*Fondsenreglement*) were completely revised in 1983 to implement the provisions of three EC Directives.

There are separate rules relating to the requirements for listing on the Parallel Market (*Reglement houdende bepalingen inzake de toelating van fondsen tot de Parallelmarkt*).

They set out, *inter alia*, the detailed requirements that apply to prospectus, obligations of listed (also referred to as issuing) institutions and the procedure for application for listing.

There are plans to integrate the rules for the Official Market and those for the Parallel Market into one rulebook on the requirements for listing on both markets. Although the requirements for listing on the Parallel Market will be tightened, they will remain less stringent than those for listing on the Official Market.

Application for admission
An application for admission of securities for listing must be submitted to the Stock Exchange Association. This applies to both official listing and listing on the Parallel Market. The application must be signed and submitted by at least one member of the Stock Exchange Association. Until the Act on the supervision of the secruties trade comes into force, the authority

to admit securities for listing is vested with the Minister of Finance. Since 1 February 1989 the Securities Board has exercised this authority on behalf of the Minister. The Act on the supervision of the securities trade leads to repeal of the statutory basis of the Minister's authority. Under the new Act the Stock Exchange Association itself will decide on admission for listing.

Prospectus

Securities are not admitted before a prospectus, approved by the Stock Exchange Association, is published. In practice, a draft prospectus is submitted to the Stock Exchange Association which checks whether all applicable requirements are complied with.

Listing agreement

The issuing institution must enter into a listing agreement with the Stock Exchange Association. Pursuant to the listing agreement the issuing institution must comply with the rules and regulations of the ASE and publish relevant financial information.

Disclosure of major shareholding

There used to be only an obligation for the issuing institution to disclose to the Stock Exchange Association and publish the name(s) of the holder(s) of a shareholding of 20 per cent or more of its capital or a change in such shareholding as soon as it became aware of such (change of) shareholding. The relevant rules have changed upon the coming into force of the Act on disclosure of holdings in listed companies. See section **1.5.7**.

Bearer securities

Although admission of registered securities for listing on the Official Market is not altogether excluded, as a general rule only bearer securities are admitted for such listing. In the past, registered securities have occasionally been admitted for listing on the Parallel Market.

Admissible securities

The rules relating to the requirements for listing on the Official Market of the ASE and the rules for the Parallel Market do not actually define 'securities'. Both sets of rules do, however, contain a list of the types of securities that may be admitted for listing:

shares; bonds (including bonds in tap-issues, such as (eg) bonds issued by mortgage banks (*pandbrieven*), bank bonds (*bankbrieven*), savings bonds (*spaarbrieven*) and savings notes (*spaarbiljetten*); convertible bonds; warrants; participation certificates; 'claims' (= rights of subscription); 'scrips' (= scrip) and vouchers which confer the right to a distribution in other securities, such as dividend vouchers earmarked for stock dividends and similar documents; and depository receipts and provisional certificates (*recepissen*) and, further, all documents that, in accordance with the general views held in business practice in the country where the issuing institution is established or in the Netherlands, as the case may be, are regarded as such.

The enumeration is not exhaustive. The words 'all documents that ... etc' have been included to make it possible that other, 'new' types of securities are listed. Fairly recent examples of new financing instruments which have been admitted for listing are the so-called FALCONS (Fixed term Agreements for Long-term Call Options on Netherlands Securities), FASCONS (Fixed term Agreements for Short-term Call Options on Netherlands Securities) and LIONS (Leveraged Income Obligations via New Shares).

Securities traded

At present, the following main types of securities are traded on the ASE:

Official Market	*Parallel Market*
shares (domestic and foreign)	shares
including claims and warrants	bonds
depository receipts of shares	
bonds, including government	
and mortgage bonds	
eurobonds	
participation certificates	
convertible bonds	

In connection with warrants it should be noted that, as a general rule, only traditional warrants are admitted for listing on the ASE; this means warrants which entitle the holders to receive new shares in the company that has issued the warrants. Certain products, although they are called 'warrants', such as put-warrants on an index, may be more suitable for listing on the European Options Exchange (see section **5.4**).

Official Price List

Prices are published in the Official Price List. Since 1987 there is a joint Official Price List for the ASE, the European Options Exchange and the Financial Futures Market Amsterdam.

5.3.3   MEMBERSHIP OF THE STOCK EXCHANGE ASSOCIATION

Two types of members

To be able to conduct business on the ASE, it is necessary to become a member of the Stock Exchange Association.

There are two types of member:
(1)   Corporate Members (*Bedrijfsleden*);
(2)   Exchange Members (*Beursleden*).

Corporate Members

Only Corporate Members can actually trade on the ASE. Corporate Members are companies and other legal entities which, as their main business or as an important part of their business, act as stockbrokers and/or trade in securities for their own account in the Netherlands.

Exchange Members

Exchange Members are natural persons who act as managing partners or managing directors of Corporate Members. Natural persons who have been appointed by Corporate Members as substitutes for their managing partners or directors for the purpose of the Exchange Membership may also be admitted as Exchange Members. The Exchange Membership is personal and linked to the office of managing partner or director with a Corporate Member.

Banks; brokers; stockjobbers

Corporate Members are further distinguished as follows:
(1)   those which, as their main business, carry on the business of stockbroking and/or trade in securities for their own account but which are not entered in one of the registers held by the Dutch Central Bank (*De Nederlandsche Bank*) pursuant to the Act on the supervision of the credit system (see Chapter 4);

(2) those which, as an important part of their business, carry on the business of stockbroking as stockbrokers or banks and/ or trade in securities for their own account and which are entered in one of the registers referred to above;

(3) those which, exclusively for the account of other members, carry on the business of stockbroking as (stock)jobbers (*hoeklieden*) and which trade in securities for their own account.

Corporate Members cannot belong to more than one of these three categories. They may trade on the exchange themselves, being represented by an Exchange Member, or they may not do so but trade exclusively through the intermediary of another Corporate Member (other than a stockjobber).

Application for membership

The written application for admittance as a member must be addressed to the Management Board of the Stock Exchange Association. It must contain details on the envisaged activities of the applicant (and thus the relevant type of membership that is applied for) and it must be accompanied by certain documents, described in the Membership Regulations (*Ledenreglement*), which show that the requirements for the relevant type of membership are complied with.

The Board is advised by the Reviewing Committee (*Toetsingscommissie*). The applicant may have to submit additional information to the Reviewing Committee. If the Board considers the applicant fit for admission as a member, it will inform all members of the Stock Exchange Association of the application by way of a circular letter. The members may, within two weeks from the day of dispatch of the circular letter, file objections against the application with the Board. The Membership Regulations contain further provisions on the objections procedure.

If the applicant is not admitted as a member he may inform the Board that he does not accept the Board's decision. The Board will then notify the Committee of Appeal (*Commissie van Beroep*) which will decide whether the applicant may be admitted as a member.

If the applicant is admitted as a member, the membership begins after the applicant has signed the register of members, by which he submits to the Articles of Association and the various rules and regulations of the Stock Exchange Association, and after payment of the admission fee and of the subscription for the current year.

Membership requirements

The requirements for membership are set out in the Articles of Association of the Stock Exchange Association and the Membership Regulations.

To obtain Corporate Membership the companies and legal entities must:

(1) have been incorporated under the law of an EC Member State;

(2) have at least two managing partners or directors, at least one of whom must be resident of or established in the Netherlands;

(3) have their (principal) office in the Netherlands;

(4) comply with the requirements relating to expertise, trustworthiness, financial resources and independence which are set out in detail in the Membership Regulations.

The application for Corporate Membership must be accompanied by the application for Exchange Membership of the managing partner(s) or director(s). If the managing partner or director of the Corporate Member is a legal entity, the Exchange Membership cannot be granted to this legal entity itself, but only to a natural person who is a director of the legal entity.

Self-regulation

Self-regulation has traditionally been an important feature of the exchange business in the Netherlands. The Stock Exchange Association has adopted its own detailed rules relating to—*inter alia*—organisation and membership, disputes, appeal, (admission for) listing and the trade on the floor.

There is a Control Department (*Controlebureau*) that looks after compliance with the articles of association and the other rules and regulations of the Stock Exchange Association. The Stock Exchange Association also has its own disciplinary board (*Commissie van Orde*). This board decides on complaints made against a member by a commission of delegates which acts of its own motion or at the request of another member. A separate commission decides on disputes between Corporate Members (*Commissie voor de Geschillen*). There is also a Commission of

Appeal (*Commissie van Beroep*) and various other permanent bodies, the members of which are appointed by the Management Board of the Stock Exchange Association.

The Committee of Good Offices (*Klachtencommissie Effectenbedrijf*) decides on complaints made against a member of the Stock Exchange Association by any person who has been directly affected by an action (or the lack of action) of such member. The parties must accept the decision of the Committee of Good Offices as binding.

5.3.4 TRADING, CLEARING, CUSTODY AND ADMINISTRATION

Method of trading

Provisions relating to trading on the Official Market of the ASE are set out in the Regulations for the Securities Trade (*Reglement voor de Effectenhandel*). These regulations deal with two subjects:

(1)　the way in which transactions are concluded; and
(2)　the rights and obligations of the parties to such transactions.

The Regulations for the trade on the Parallel Market are virtually the same.

Introduction of orders

On the Official Market customers may introduce orders with any Corporate Member of the Stock Exchange Association except (stock)jobbers. A (stock)jobber is only allowed to act as intermediary between other Corporate Members of the Stock Exchange Association. A (stock)jobber is not allowed to have direct relations with the investors.

On the Parallel Market brokers have to introduce their orders to either one of the two 'specialists' on the Parallel Market who substantially have the same role as the (stock)jobbers on the Official Market.

Fondsen

Trading takes place in *fondsen*, specific categories of securities issued by one and the same issuing institution which confer on all the holders' rights which are, in proportion to their interest in the *fonds*, equal as between them.

Hoek

A *fonds* is traded in a particular section of the floor (*hoek*) where the market in that *fonds* is made by the (stock)jobbers. In a *hoek* at least two jobbers compete in trading the *fonds*. On the basis of orders received from banks and brokers, the (stock)jobbers determine the price. All jobbers in the same *fonds* must agree on that price. The information on transactions concluded at that price is immediately reported by the (stock)jobbers for dissemination on the floor and worldwide through data communication systems.

Trade Support System

In September 1988 the Trade Support System (*Handel Ondersteunend Systeem*) was officially put in place.

In the Trade Support System the banks and brokers may place orders by entering them into their computers. The orders appear on their computer screens on the floor and in their offices outside the stock exchange building. A dealer may send an order directly to the order book of the (stock)jobber on his screen. The (stock)jobber will, together with his competitors, set a new price on the basis of the orders thus appearing in his order book. Execution of all orders which fit this price takes place automatically. The Trade Support System is connected with price dissemination and clearing and settlement systems (see below). Through the Trade Support System the parties involved can at all times see which orders are open, which trades have been completed and what are the positions within several listed *fondsen*. The Trade Support System includes a position prognosis feature which enables the (stock)jobbers to establish what their order book would look like at several different prospective prices.

AIM

The Amsterdam Interprofessional Market System (AIM), which became fully operational in January 1987, opens the possibility for banks and brokers to negotiate prices and to conclude transactions directly with clients without the intermediary of the (stock)jobbers. AIM only operates for securities listed on the Official Market. The transactions must have an effective value of at least Dfl1m (for shares) or Dfl2.5m (for bonds and convertible bonds).

However, transactions between banks and brokers themselves still require the intermediary of the jobbers on the floor.

Open Order Book

In July 1990 a new system for wholesale trading in Dutch government bonds was launched. This system is called Open Order Book. Brokers can put limit orders into the system with a minimum amount of Dfl2.5m. Brokers who act as market makers can enter quotes (bid and offer prices) in the system, with a minimum amount of Dfl5m. Through a (stock)jobber acting as 'interdealer broker', the brokers can conclude transactions on the basis of the orders and quotes entered in the Open Order Book.

Securities Clearing Corporation

Generally, all transactions in officially listed securities are settled via the Securities Clearing Corporation (*Effectenclearing BV*), which is a wholly-owned subsidiary of the Stock Exchange Association.

The Corporate Members, unless they have expressly agreed otherwise, must settle all their transactions in securities which have been admitted to the Effectenclearing (ie the system operated by the Securities Clearing Corporation) through the Securities Clearing Corporation, for which purpose Corporate Members are required to participate in the Effectenclearing.

The Management Board of the Stock Exchange Association decides which securities within the meaning of the Act on securities transactions by giro (*Wet giraal effectenverkeer*) are delivered to or by the Securities Clearing Corporation by way of giro transfer, a book-entry system more fully described below.

If the transaction relates to a *fonds* which has not been admitted to the Effectenclearing or if the parties have expressly excluded settlement of a transaction through the Effectenclearing and have also excluded delivery by giro, delivery takes place at the offices of the transferee. However, in practice this is hardly ever the case.

The Securities Clearing Corporation processes the transactions that have been concluded on the floor and that have been automatically passed on through the Trade Support System. The Securities Clearing Corporation confirms the transactions to the parties. It then becomes the counterparty of the buyer and the seller and guarantees delivery and payment.

On every business day, the Securities Clearing Corporation balances or 'nets' the purchases and sales of the members. The members will have positions to receive and to deliver securities. Settlement is effected by delivering securities to the Securities Clearing Corporation. The securities are then forwarded by the Securities Clearing Corporation. This is done through Necigef (see below).

The Securities Clearing Corporation also initiates the cash settlement through Kas-Associatie (see below).

Giro transfer

As indicated above, there is a system of securities' transfers by giro based on the Act on securities transactions by giro (WGE) of 8 June 1977. The WGE has simplified the transactions in securities because there is no physical delivery of certificates but securities are transferred by way of 'giro' transfer, a book-entry system. The WGE also provides for a more practical form of custody.

Necigef

Investors deposit their securities with one of the participants in Necigef, the Netherlands Central Securities Giro Institute (*Nederlands Centraal Instituut voor Giraal Effectenverkeer*). In the WGE the participants are referred to as 'affiliated institutions' (*aangesloten instellingen*). At present, affiliated institutions are the Dutch Central Bank, a large number of banks and a few other institutions (including similar foreign institutions), such as the Securities Clearing Corporation.

Collective depots

Each participant holds separate 'collective depots' (*verzamel-depots*) for different types of securities. The participants are charged with the administration of the collective depots held by them.

Placing securities into custody with a participant results in the investor becoming co-owner of the collective depot together with all the other investors in the same kind of securities. The investor's share in the collective depot is calculated pro-rata to the number of the securities placed into custody. The investor is entitled to receive back from the affiliated institution the same number of securities as he has placed into custody, but he is not entitled to receive back exactly the same certificates of the securities.

It is possible to transfer (or pledge) (part of) a share (by which is meant here the co-ownership) in a collective depot. Delivery takes place by way of book-entry in the relevant part of the affiliated institution's administration.

Central 'giro depot'

The participants deposit part of the collective depots with Necigef, the central depository. Necigef holds a central *giro* depot for each type of security. Necigef is both custodian and administrator and is supervised by the Minister of Finance through an appointed supervisor. Only participants can place securities into custody with Necigef. The provisions of the WGE on co-ownership of central *giro* depots and on transfer and pledging of a share in a central *giro* depot are—in broad terms— similar to those relating to collective depots. The giro depots form part of the collective depots.

The Management Board of Necigef has adopted a set of detailed rules on the deposit into Necigef's central *giro* depots, the custody and administration and related matters.

K or CF-certificates

Bearer securities may exist in K or CF-form. CF is the abbreviation of Centre for Fund Administration BV (*Centrum voor Fondsenadministratie BV*) which administers the balances of its participants. The Centre for Fund Administration was set up to create a system in which it would not be necessary to present a physical instrument to claim distributions on the securities like dividends and interest.

Share certificates to bearer consist of two parts, one is the share certificate itself (*mantel*) and the other is a sheet consisting of dividend coupons and a so-called *talon* or is simply one dividend sheet. The share certificates to bearer which consist of a *mantel* and such a singular dividend sheet are called CF-certificates. The share certificates to bearer which consist of a *mantel* and a dividend sheet which itself is composed of several dividend coupons and a so-called *talon* are called K-certificates. The importance of K-certificates has decreased since the introduction of CF-certificates.

Necigef only accepts the (CF) certificates if the securities are eligible for the giro system. Virtually all *fondsen* listed in the Official Price List have been admitted to the giro system. Delivery of these securities is effected by book-entry. The selling party instructs Necigef to debit its account in a certain security and to credit the account of Securities Clearing Corporation with Necigef. Necigef advises the Securities Clearing Corporation which, in turn, informs Necigef of the buying party. The account of the buying party is then credited and the whole process is completed.

If the securities are not admitted to the giro system, *physical* delivery has to take place through Kas-Associatie, in which case the Securities Clearing Corporation only accepts delivery in CF-form.

If the securities only exist in K-form, there are two possibilities:

(1) the securities are admitted to Necigef: the delivery takes place as with CF-certificates by book-entry within Necigef;

(2) the securities are not admitted to Necigef: the selling party physically delivers the securities to Kas-Associatie which informs the Effectenclearing which, in turn, credits and debits the accounts of the parties involved.

NIEC

The duties of the central securities depositary are in the process of being extended to put a nominee function in place. To achieve this the Netherlands Interprofessional Securities Centre (*Nederlands Interprofessioneel Effecten Centrum*; NIEC) has been established. NIEC is a 'sister' institution of Necigef.

Kas-Associatie

The *financial* settlement takes place through Kas-Associatie which is a 60 per cent subsidiary company of the Stock Exchange Association. All members of the Stock Exchange Association maintain a cash account with Kas-Associatie. The Securities Clearing Corporation ascertains delivery against payment by simultaneously effecting the delivery of securities through Necigef and the payment of the corresponding price through Kas-Associatie. The Securities Clearing Corporation provides information to Kas-Associatie on the cash consideration for securities delivered and received for the members. Kas-Associatie then debits and credits the accounts of the members accordingly.

Delivery versus payment

In 1990 the ASE took two measures to improve the 'delivery *versus* payment' system. The first was the introduction of the fixed settlement date. Delivery of the securities must take place on the seventh day after the transaction has been concluded. The fixed settlement date has enabled the use of a system of automatic securities collection. This means that a member can instruct the Securities Clearing Corporation to debit the securities account of the member at Necigef for a delivery obligation of the member towards the Securities Clearing Corporation. The member itself then does not have to instruct Necigef.

The second measure was the implementation of the 'same day fund' principle, ie the simultaneous exchange of securities and payment for securities.

5.3.5 ASAS

Introduction

ASAS used to be the abbreviation of American Shares Amsterdam System. The system was set up in 1980 to solve the problems which had arisen in the trade on the ASE of depositary receipts to bearer of American registered shares, listed on the New York Stock Exchange.

Since 1980 similar systems have been developed for the trade on the ASE in other foreign securities. These systems are collectively referred to as Amsterdam Security Account System, also abbreviated ASAS.

Main features of ASAS

Foreign securities are deposited with Nominee Amsterdam Stock Exchange NV (*Nominee*) on the basis of a deposit agreement. Depositors must also enter into an agreement with ASAS Servicing Company NV. The most important categories of participants in the system are members of the Stock Exchange Association, credit institutions and members of foreign stock exchanges which are members of the *Fédération Internationale des Bourses de Valeur* (International Federation of Stock Exchanges).

Delivery of securities to Nominee and of deposited securities by Nominee is not governed by Dutch law as this takes place through a custodian outside the Netherlands.

For the deposit of securities with Nominee, the depositor is credited in the books of Nominee. Nominee issues to the depositor a registered depositary receipt that is not embodied in any document. The depositor's credit balance at Nominee is generally referred to as 'an ASAS'. 'ASAS' are listed on the ASE and traded on the floor.

Settlement of ASAS transactions

The settlement of ASAS transactions takes place through Nominee and ASAS Servicing Company NV. Delivery only takes place by book transfer within Nominee according to the settlement procedures of the home market. For each ASAS security recorded in the books of Nominee, an actual security is deposited with the depository located in the home country. Financial settlement takes place through Kas-Associatie.

5.4 EUROPEAN OPTIONS EXCHANGE

5.4.1 INTRODUCTION

In 1978 the Amsterdam Stock Exchange took the initiative to establish the European Options Exchange (EOE), the first options exchange in Europe.

Organisation

Economically speaking, the Association European Options Exchange (*Association EOE*) is the owner of the entire options exchange, the clearing corporations and all related business. The Association EOE is a holding the participations of which are divided into two categories:
(1) the companies involved in the trade;
(2) the companies involved in the clearing and settlement.

The actual organiser of the options exchange is Options Exchange NV (*Optiebeurs NV*), a wholly-owned subsidiary of Association EOE.

Association EOE also holds the entire share capital of the clearing holding European Options Clearing Corporation BV (EOCC). This company not only holds shares in the capital of the various companies involved in the clearing and settlement on the EOE, but is also shareholder of the EFCC, European Futures

Clearing Corporation BV, the clearing company for the Financial
Futures Market Amsterdam (see section **5.5**).

Options traded
    At present, the following option categories are traded on the
EOE:
(1)   share-options;
(2)   bond-options;
(3)   currency-options;
(4)   precious metal options;
(5)   index-options (options on the EOE Dutch share index, the
       Major Market Index and the Eurotop 100 Index); and
(6)   future-options (options with respect to future bonds).
       There are two types of options·
(1)   put options; and
(2)   call options.

5.4.2   PARTICIPANTS IN THE TRADE ON THE EOE

    Participants in the trade on the EOE are:
(1)   the investors;
(2)   the Public Order Members;
(3)   the Remisiers;
(4)   the Public Order Correspondent Members;
(5)   the Floor Brokers;
(6)   the Clearing Corporations;
(7)   the Market Makers;
(8)   the Off Floor Traders and Floor Broker Specialists.

Investors
    The investors, private persons but also large institutional
investors, instigate the process of the options trade.

Public Order Members
    Public Order Members (POMs) are members of the
Association EOE and can be compared to stockbrokers on the
Amsterdam Stock Exchange. They are entitled to accept orders
from customers for the conclusion of option transactions for the
account of such customers.
    POMs must have an EOE 'seat' type A; this is in fact a
registered A-share in the capital of Association EOE.

To execute their customers' orders, the POMs are dependent on Floor Brokers.

Remisiers

Remisiers are not members of the Association EOE. Pursuant to a contractual relationship with POMs or Public Order Correspondent Members they are entitled to solicit new clients or orders from existing clients against payment by the POMs or Public Order Correspondent Members of a certain fee. Although remisiers are not EOE members the EOE does exercise a certain form of supervision in respect of remisiers.

Public Order Correspondent Members

Public Order Correspondent Members are members of Association EOE with a 'seat' type B but their activities do not differ much from those of remisiers. Orders received from clients are passed on to POMs which, in their turn, pass these orders on to Floor Brokers.

Floor Brokers

Floor Brokers are members of Association EOE with a 'seat' type A. They are exclusively authorised to execute the orders received from the POMs in option trades on the floor (for the account of the POMs). Floor Brokers are virtually always legal entities. Their employees are the actual traders on the floor.

Clearing Members

Clearing Members are also members of Association EOE with a 'seat' type A. All trades are in fact 'attributed' to the Clearing Members; the Clearing Members eventually become parties to the option transactions which they may enter into in their own name and for the account and at the instructions of POMs, Floor Brokers (and Off Floor Traders) and Market Makers or for their own account. Such option transactions are concluded with the Clearing Corporations.

Clearing Corporations

The Clearing Corporations are not members of Association EOE. If an investor has given instructions to purchase a certain option, this will result in the Clearing Member purchasing the option from the Clearing Corporation.

Market Makers

The Market Makers, like the Floor Brokers, are traders on the floor. They are members of Association EOE and have a 'seat' type A. They make a market in specific categories of options to which they are assigned. Market Makers may conclude transactions on the EOE for their own account.

Application for membership

Both natural persons and legal entities may apply for membership. The application for membership must be submitted to the Management Board of the Association EOE. The application procedure is further set out in the Rules for Members. The applicant has to state in which capacity or capacities (POM, Public Order Correspondent Member, Floor Broker, Clearing Member, Market Maker) he or it wants to become a member.

Membership requirements

For each capacity the Articles of Association of Association EOE set out the requirements that have to be met to be admitted as a member in that capacity. The membership requirements relate to financial safeguards, expertise, trustworthiness and morality, business conduct, activities, qualifications, legal status, office, equity, independence and, for POMs and Public Order Correspondent Members, the providing of information to the public.

Self-regulation

Like the ASE, the European Options Exchange has also adopted its own detailed rules and regulations relating to all aspects of the options trade. It also has its own departments and committees to deal with compliance with the rules and regulations, disputes, appeals etc. The Committee of Good Offices of the ASE also acts as Committee of Good Offices of the EOE.

5.4.3 TRADE ON THE FLOOR

The investor instructs a POM to conclude a certain option transaction. The POM passes the order on to Floor Brokers. Floor Brokers may either be employed by the POM or be independent companies which employ their own people who can act on the floor. A large number of banks and brokers also act as Floor Brokers.

Having received orders in a particular category of options, the Floor Brokers go to the *posts* where the trade in that category takes place among Floor Brokers and Market Makers. As soon as a transaction has been concluded, the transaction details are reported through automated systems on the EOE floor and worldwide. The transaction details are forwarded to the Trade Matching department. At the end of a business day the necessary details are sent to the Clearing Corporations so that the clearing and settlement process is set in motion.

5.5 FINANCIAL FUTURES MARKET AMSTERDAM

In 1987 the European Options Exchange took the initiative for the establishment of a market for the trade in financial futures, the Financial Futures Market Amsterdam (the FFMA). Given the scope of this book, the FFMA will only be described very briefly.

Organisation

The market is organised by FFMA NV. To be able to carry on business on the FFMA it is necessary to have a seat as Clearing Member, Broker, Trader or Market Maker. The capacities of Broker and Market Maker may not be combined. Applications for seats must be made with the FFMA in accordance with the requirements set out in the rules and regulations of the FFMA.

Self-regulation

The FFMA is also operated on the basis of the principle of self-regulation. There are General Regulations, Trading Rules, Announcements on—*inter alia*—futures contract specifications, costs, position and exercise limits. The European Futures Clearing Corporation BV clears futures transactions on the conditions set out in the General Conditions EFCC. The Committee of Good Offices of the European Options Exchange also acts as Committee of Good Offices of the FFMA.

Futures traded

At present, the following types of futures are traded:
(1) bond futures;

(2)   'fti'contacts (1 future contract = Dfl200 × the EOE Share Index);

(3)   Dutch top 5 index futures;

(4)   futures on the Eurotop 100 Index; and

(5)   US Dollar/Guilder futures.

5.6   INSIDER DEALING

Criminal sanction

Insider dealing is covered by the provisions of art 336a of the Dutch Criminal Code which came into force on 16 February 1989.

A person having inside information may not conclude or procure the conclusion of transactions in securities which are listed on exchanges which are supervised by the Dutch Government, if a certain advantage may result from the transaction. The penalty is a maximum term of imprisonment of two years and a maximum fine of Dfl100,000 or Dfl1m in the case of a legal entity or one of these penalties. In addition the estimated gains from the illegal action may be claimed back.

The same penalties could be imposed on a person who, from within the Netherlands and having inside information, procures a transaction in securities which are listed on a stock exchange outside the Netherlands, if a certain advantage may result from the transaction.

Inside information is defined as knowledge of a particular fact concerning a legal entity or company to which the securities relate, or knowledge of a particular fact concerning the trade in these securities:

(1)   in respect of which the person who is aware of the particular fact knows, or should reasonably know, that it is not public and that it cannot or may not leave the circle of those who have a confidentiality obligation with respect to it without a breach of such confidentiality obligation; and

(2)   disclosure of which, as may be reasonably expected, will affect the price of the securities.

The prohibition does not apply to an intermediary who, exclusively having inside information with respect to the trade, trades on the exchange in accordance with the principle of good faith to serve his principal.

Model Code Stock Exchange Association

On 1 January 1987 the Stock Exchange Association had, in anticipation of a general statutory regulation, already issued a 'Model Code to Prevent Insider Dealing'. This code is annexed to the rules relating to the requirements for listing on the Offical Market of the Amsterdam Stock Exchange. A similar regulation is applicable to the Parallel Market. The code provides for imposing various obligations and prohibitions upon the listed institution to prevent insider trading. This takes place in the listing agreement between the Stock Exchange Association and the listed institution. The main rule is that the managing directors, supervisory directors and designated key employees of the listed institution are not permitted to trade in the securities of this institution if they have knowledge of facts which may have an effect on the price.

During certain specified periods of time the prohibition applies irrespective of whether one has price-sensitive information.

The Stock Exchange Association may take various measures upon breach of any of the obligations or prohibitions imposed upon the listed institution in the listing agreement; the breach may be made public and also listing measures may be taken.

The prohibitions and restrictions of the Model Code are also applicable to the trade in options on the relevant securities on the European Options Exchange.

Other ASE rules

The Membership Regulations and the Code of Conduct for securities transactions (*Gedragscode voor effectentransacties*) also contain provisions which have as their object the prevention of insider trading.

Regulation in the Merger Code

Rules to prevent insider dealing have also been included in the Merger Code of the Social and Economic Council (see Chapter 4).

Each managing and supervisory director of each of the NVs involved in a firm public offer is obliged to submit to the Committee for Merger Affairs (see **Introduction**), together with the publication of the notice of offer, a detailed review of the dealings effected by himself, his spouse, his minor children and by legal entities of which these persons have the control, during the six months prior to the first public announcement regarding the price or exchange ratio:

(1)   in shares of the offeree NV; and

(2)   if the offer exclusively or partly relates to the take-over of shares in exchange for shares to be issued by the offeror NV, in shares issued by the offeror NV.

Every managing or supervisory director of the offeree NV shall submit to the Committee for Merger Affairs, simultaneously with the publication of the notice of offer, a detailed review of the number and the kind of shares issued by the offeree NV, which are held by him, his spouse, his minor children or by legal entities of which these persons have the control.

Similar obligations apply to each managing and supervisory director of each of the NVs involved in a partial or tender offer.

If this regulation in the Merger Rules is breached the Social and Economic Council may issue a public condemnation or publish the breach of the regulation.

With a view to the necessity of upholding confidence in the financial markets in the Netherlands and of staying in line with developments in other countries, the non-statutory regulations of the Stock Exchange Association and the Social and Economic Council were 'complemented' by the general criminal sanction of art 336a.

EC

An EC Directive on insider dealing was adopted by the EC Council on 13 November 1989. It is not expected that the directive will lead to important changes in the Dutch legislation on insider dealing.

ASST

It is proposed to (slightly) redraft the present provisions of the Criminal Code on insider dealing and to include them in the Act on the supervision of the securities trade (see section **5.1**). This will render insider dealing an economic offence under the Economic Offences Act. It is expected that this will facilitate investigation and prosecution of suspected insider dealing.

5.7 THE BORROWING AND LENDING OF SECURITIES

General

In recent years the interest in the possibility of borrowing and lending securities in the Netherlands has considerably increased. However, the market for borrowing and lending securities in the Netherlands would still seem to be less developed than the market for such borrowing and lending in some other countries, such as England.

Qualification

There are, at present, no specific rules and regulations on the borrowing and lending of securities. The agreement for the borrowing and lending of securities can (usually) be qualified as an 'agreement for a loan for consumption' (*verbruikleenovereenkomst*) under Dutch law. A 'loan for consumption' is an agreement whereby one party (the lender) lends to the other party (the borrower) a certain sum of money or a certain quantity of other replaceable goods, and whereby the borrower is obliged to return an equal sum of money or quantity of goods of the same sort and of the same quality. Under the present Dutch civil law a 'loan for consumption' is an agreement which only comes into existence by delivery of the relevant goods to which the agreement relates. Such an agreement is referred to as a *reëel* agreement. Under the New Dutch Civil Code a 'loan for consumption' is not a *reëel* agreement; it is created by agreement between the parties. It is not necessary for the creation of the agreement that the goods are delivered. Such an agreement is known as a *consensueel* agreement. When the relevant part of (Book 7 of) the New Dutch Civil Code comes into force, this will not have to result in a complete change of the standardised contracts for the borrowing and lending of securities. Only a further regulation, relating to the point in time on which the agreement is created, will be necessary.

Main market participants

The main lenders of securities in the Netherlands are Kas-Associatie, the major clearing banks and institutional investors. The main borrowers of securities in the Netherlands are market makers on the European Options Exchange and brokers.

Central lending facility ASE

There have been plans for introducing a central lending facility on the Amsterdam Stock Exchange. The plans for this facility, announced as the Interprofessional Equalisation Depot, are at present reconsidered as the original plans seem to have failed in attracting lenders' interest.

Future

The market for borrowing and lending securities in the Netherlands is developing. The participants in the market will consider new structures and mechanics to improve their position. In due course (further) regulations may be expected with a view to the increasing volume of borrowing and lending activities and the increasing number of market participants.

6
UNFAIR COMPETITION AND INTELLECTUAL PROPERTY LAW

6.1 INTRODUCTION

In view of the scope of this book it is impossible to give a complete survey of the Dutch law of unfair competition and intellectual property. A selection has been made of the most important provisions which a company doing business in or with the Netherlands could come across. We have decided not to deal with the Semiconductors Act (*Wet houdende regelen inzake de bescherming van oorspronkelijke topografieën van halfgeleider produkten*), which is in conformity with the EC directive of 16 December 1986 (Official Journal 1987 L24) and the Plant Variety Act (*Zaaizaad en Plantgoed Wet*).

We have almost entirely refrained from remarks about the impact of European Community law as information on this is sufficiently available in more widely spoken languages than Dutch.

6.2 UNFAIR COMPETITION

6.2.1 INTRODUCTION

Dutch law does not have a specific Act dealing with unfair competition. The unfair competition law has been based on art 1401 of the old Civil Code and the interpretation given to this article by the Supreme Court in its Lindenbaum/Cohen decision 1919.

Article 6:162 sub 2 of the New Civil Code which came into force on 1 January 1992 contains the same interpretation and reads as follows:

The following is considered a tort:

(a) infringement of a right;

(b) acting, or failing to act, contrary to a legal obligation; or
(c) acting, or failing to act, contrary to what is, under unwritten law, proper behaviour in society (comparable to the English concept of 'duty of care').

Infringement of a right

The category 'infringement of a right' is in fact dealt with in respect of special subjects in the different Acts such as the Patent Act, the Benelux Trademark Act etc. These Acts give the inventor, the trademark owner etc certain rights. Infringement of such rights is very often prohibited by provisions of the Act itself and in these cases art 6:162 sub 2 does not play a role. However, art 6:162 sub 2 does become relevant in instances in which a specific Act does not contain such prohibitive provisions. If and to what extent art 6:162 sub 2 can provide additional rights depends in fact on the nature of the additional right claimed and the nature of the Act under which such additional right is sought.

Acting, or failing to act, contrary to a legal obligation

First, it should be noted that this category and the previous (infringement of a right) cannot always be strictly separated. The Patent Act, for instance, contains, in addition to certain 'rights', criminal provisions which create a legal obligation not to infringe those rights. Acting against such legal obligations constitutes an act of tort.

Furthermore, it should be noted that many legal obligations are not written for the protection of competitors but for another purpose. A competitor cannot obtain relief on the basis of art 6:162 sub 2 if the legal obligation concerned does not have the purpose of protecting competitors. This does not exclude the possibility that acting contrary to this legal obligation (which is not written to protect the competitor) is, at the same time, acting against the 'duty of care' to a competitor.

There are many examples of legal obligations in a wide range of statutes.

In addition, the Criminal Code contains a general provision prohibiting unfair competition (art 328 *bis*) which in practice, however, is of no importance because of its scope of applicability. In practice, one therefore prefers to rely on the 'duty of care' category.

There are also many administrative Acts containing legal obligations with respect to the establishment of a business, the sales of products or the product themselves.

Important provisions are furthermore art 1416a–c of the Civil Code (arts 6:194–196 of the New Civil Code) regarding misleading advertising, which set out the possibility of acting against such advertising and which shift the burden of proof to the advertiser. In addition to these provisions in the Civil Code, there is also a self-regulatory body (with representatives of advertisers, advertising agency and consumers), the Advertisement Council (*Reclameraad*). The Advertisement Council has its own rules of conduct for advertising and deals with complaints.

Finally, a company can of course invoke before the national courts arts 85 and 86 of the EC Treaty in order to prevent its competitor from violating these articles or to obtain compensation for the damages suffered as a result of such violation.

Duty of care

This is the most important category in respect of which extensive case law has developed. The starting point, according to this case law, is the principle of freedom of trade and industry. This principle entails a basic freedom to compete even if this is detrimental to the competitor.

A competitor can, in turn, take advantage of efforts of his competitors as long as the result of such efforts is not protected under the intellectual property acts. Only under specific additional circumstances, does this taking advantage of the efforts of the competitor become unfair. One of these circumstances is causing unnecessary confusion. The emphasis here is on '*unnecessary*'. This means that the competitor must always have the possibility of giving his products and services the same advantageous properties as the products or services of the competitor, even if in doing so it causes confusion. If a competitor develops a unique advantageous selling method, every competitor can use the same selling method. If that in itself would cause confusion, this cannot be unfair competition. However, if the competitor also uses the same colours, packaging and shop interior, while this would not be necessary for taking advantage of the same selling method, there would be unfair competition if this could cause confusion.

6.2.2   PROTECTION OF ACHIEVEMENTS (*PRESTATIES*)

There is one exception to the rule that one can take advantage of (including imitate or copy) the results of the efforts of competitors without causing unnecessary confusion. For this exception to be applicable, the result of the efforts for which one claims protection must be *comparable* with performances which are protected under intellectual property acts.

This exception was successfully invoked against the unauthorised selling of Elvis Presley soundtracks. An important factor thereby was that the Netherlands were at the time in the process of passing legislation in accordance with the Rome Convention of 1966 which, *inter alia*, protects the rights of performers.

6.2.3   STATEMENTS ABOUT THE COMPETITOR

As explained above in section **6.2.1** the Civil Code contains provisons with respect to misleading advertising.

A competitor may, of course, also make statements about the products or services of his competitor or about the competitor himself.

It is not necessary to use the name of the competitor. It is sufficient that it is clear to the public that reference is made to the competitor or his product.

If untrue, such statements are always tortious. True statements will only be tortious under certain circumstances. If asked for, a true statement about the product of a competitor will not be tortious. However, if such statements are made public and have not been asked for and if they have the clear purpose of causing damages, such statements are tortious. One must furthermore realise that a statement which is in itself true may be misleading because of other true facts which are omitted.

Warning against possible infringement of intellectual property rights is allowed if the person issuing the warning acts in good faith. This good faith is not present if such person knows or should know that his allegations are unfounded.

6.2.4   COMPARATIVE ADVERTISING

Basically the same rules apply as described above in section **6.2.3**. The situation in the Netherlands with respect to comparative advertising which does not contain untrue statements is not entirely clear. This matter is complicated by art 13(A) under (2) of the Benelux Trademark Act which prohibits any use of a trademark without a 'valid reason' which may cause damages. In general, case law of the lower courts does not consider comparative advertising to be a 'valid reason' for use of a competitor's trademark.

6.3   PATENT LAW

6.3.1   INTRODUCTION

The Netherlands are party to various treaties which have the purpose of harmonising patent laws. Dutch patent law resembles, in many aspects, the patent laws in other countries, especially those which are party to the Treaty of Strasbourg 1963 and/or the European Patent Convention 1973. On the other hand, Dutch patent law contains a few peculiar aspects which it is important to be aware of. In general, one can say that during the last decade it has become somewhat easier to obtain a patent and that there is a certain tendency in the lower courts to give a more limited scope of protection. However, the Supreme Court has clearly indicated in its leading Meyn/Stork decision 1989 that it does not agree with such limitation.

One of the advantages of the Dutch patent system lies in the law of civil proceedings which in most cases provides a good, efficient and relatively inexpensive possibility of enforcement. This makes the Dutch courts attractive for international forumshopping.

Future (new Patent Act)

It is expected that within a year a new Patent Act will replace the old Patent Act (*Rijksoctrooiwet*).

The most important change will relate to the application procedure for national patents (patents not obtained via the European but via the national system). This procedure will change dramatically.

Under the present system the procedure includes a full examination by the Patent Office and—before the patent is granted—opposition possibilities for third parties. This means that the application procedure may take many years. Those years reduce the actual period of protection as the patent expires 20 years after the *date of application*.

The new Patent Act provides for two types of patents. The first type of patent will be granted without any search (apart from the checking of compliance with certain formal requirements). This patent is valid for six years after the date of application. It will be granted almost immediately after the patent application has been published, which normally takes place 18 months after the application is filed. However, one cannot invoke such patent in the courts against infringement without having first obtained a prior art search report. Alternatively, the applicant may, within 13 months after the application, request a prior art search or hand over a prior art search report based on the Patent Cooperation Treaty.

After the issue of the search report the applicant has four months to adapt his application. Thereafter a patent will be granted. This (second type of) patent will be valid for 20 years after the application has been made.

It follows that in respect of both types of patents, the Patent Office will not examine the patent on, *inter alia*, novelty and obviousness. This will only take place during infringement and/or nullity proceedings in the courts.

Treaties

The Netherlands are party to the following treaties which have provisions in the field of patents: the Treaty of Paris 1883 (as amended), the Patent Cooperation Treaty 1970, the European Patent Treaty 1973, the Treaty of Strasbourg 1963 and 1971 and the Treaty of Budapest 1977.

As early as 1959, work was started on the Community Patent Convention which was to provide for a patent covering the whole of the European Community. At the moment it is unlikely that in the foreseeable future there will be one patent covering the whole of the EC territory. It is likely, however, that in the near future a Community Patent Convention will come into force covering only a limited number of EC countries.

6.3.2 EUROPEAN VERSUS DUTCH PATENT

Dutch patent

Patent protection in the Netherlands can be obtained in two ways. In the first place one can file an application with the Dutch Patent Office and follow the national application procedure which may lead to a patent which applies in the Kingdom of the Netherlands, consisting of the Netherlands, the Netherlands Antilles and Aruba.

European patent
The other way of obtaining a patent is through the application procedure set out in the European Patent Convention. Such procedure may lead to a European patent which—assuming that in the application the Netherlands was included as 'designated country'—is valid in the Netherlands (*not* in the Netherlands Antilles and Aruba). In general, the national application procedure, instead of the European procedure, is only used by smaller Dutch companies who do not, or hardly, rely on exports.

Difference
The most important difference between the national application procedure and the European application procedure is the following. In the national application procedure, third parties have the possibility to oppose the grant *before* the grant of the patent while in the European application procedure opposition is only possible *after the grant*.

Considering the fact that under Dutch patent law an injunction against an infringer can only be obtained *after* the patent has been granted, this difference is significant as the opposition procedure may take several years.

6.3.3   REQUIREMENTS FOR OBTAINING A PATENT

In addition to formal requirements, the following material requirements have to be fulfilled in order to obtain a patent.

Novelty
The 'prior art' should not contain the product or method for which a patent is applied. In order to avoid double patenting, both the Dutch Patent Act and the European Patent Convention contain certain provisions which include in the prior art, by way of fiction, certain pending but not yet published applications.

In addition to the prior art by way of fiction, everything which was, wherever in the world, accessible to third parties before the day of the application, is part of the prior art.

Non-obviousness

The product or method for which a patent is sought should not be obvious to the average person skilled in the art. Under the influence of the case law of the European Patent Office, the Dutch Patent Office has become less strict over the years. The courts (and especially the Court of Appeal) have a tendency to be somewhat stricter.

Patentable subject matter

In general, the Dutch Patent Office follows the European Patent Convention and the case law of the European Patent Office on this point. There are, however, some exceptions. The Dutch Patent Office has a more liberal view with respect to the possibility of protection of computer programs. According to a decision of the Dutch Patent Office, a method for a new and inventive way of processing information can be protected, even if the programme does only entail numerical calculations. The European Patent Office requires that the programme carries out an essentially technical adaptation. On the other hand, contrary to the view of the European Patent Office, the Dutch Patent Office does not accept the patentability of the 'second medical indication' (the invention of a new application of an existing pharmaceutical).

Entitlement to the patent

Dutch patent law is based on the system of first filing.

The Patent Act contains, *inter alia*, a provision with respect to inventions made by employees. The provision can also be of importance for the entitlement to a European patent including the rights resulting from a European patent in countries other than the Netherlands. Dutch law will govern this question if the employee, who is the inventor of the subject matter of the European patent, is primarily employed in the Netherlands or, if it is not clear in which country he is primarily employed, if the company by which he is employed is established in the Netherlands.

Dutch law provides that the employer is entitled to the inventions made by an employee if such invention falls within the scope of work for which the employee was hired. If the employee cannot be considered to have received compensation for the invention in his salary, he is entitled to a reasonable reward.

Scope of protection

The Patent Act contains in art 30 under 2 the same provision as art 69 under 1 of the European Patent Convention. Article 30 under 2 reads:

> The exclusive right is determined by the contents of the claims of the patent, whereby the description and the drawings serve as an explanation of those claims.

The Dutch Supreme Court has considered in its Meyn/Stork decision of 1989 that 'the essence of the patented invention' must be the starting point for the establishment of the scope of protection. The essence of the patented invention can be found by establishing (by study of the patent and the file of the application procedure) which problem the invention solves and on which 'inventive thought' such solution is based.

Each application of this 'inventive thought' for the solution of the same problem will be considered use of the essence of the patented invention. If the text of the claims does not literally cover such use of the essence of the patented invention, third parties will not infringe the patent only if they had good grounds to rely on the literal text.

Forbidden acts

In practice, a patentee can prohibit:

(1) the use of patented methods;
(2) the manufacture of and all commercial acts with respect to patented products; and
(3) the manufacture of and all commercial acts with respect to products which directly result from the use of a patented method.

The patentee can also act against certain indirect infringements such as the sale of essential parts, not being staple articles, which are suitable and destined for the application of the invention in the Netherlands.

Rights conferred by the patent application

Until the patent has been granted, the patentee cannot invoke his patent application in order to obtain an injunction.

However, once the patent is granted, the patentee has the right to reasonable compensation and/or to payment of damages with respect to the period *before* the patent was granted. In order to claim such compensation or damages it is necessary to issue a writ (the *desbewustheidsexploit*) in which the patentee informs the party which makes use of his invention about the patent application and indicates to this party which actions he considers to be within the scope of such application. Such writ should be issued as soon as possible after the party who uses the invention described in the patent application has started to use the invention.

If the patentee wants to claim damages for infringements of his patent after the grant of the patent, the patentee should also issue such a writ in order to be sure that he will be entitled to damages.

Exhaustion

Dutch patent law contains the system of national exhaustion. Therefore, the patentee can prevent import into the Netherlands of products which have been put on the market outside the European Community by him or with his consent. Within the European Community such imports cannot be prevented because of the overriding principle of the free flow of products (compare, *inter alia*, the EC Court of Justice Centrafarm decision of 1975).

Limitation on rights

The Patent Act contains provisions with respect to 'prior use'. After the grant of the patent to a third party, the prior user in the Netherlands can continue his use and all use which does not entail a new inventive step in comparison with his use prior to the date of the patent application of such third party.

The patentee furthermore has to accept 'compulsory licences' in, *inter alia*, the following events:

(1)   if such licence is required by the public interest. Such licence is granted by the Minister of Economic Affairs;

(2)   in case of non exploitation of the invention without good reason within three years after the grant of the patent;

(3)   if the licence is necessary in order to be able to exploit a younger patent, against which younger patent—in the case of a European patent—no opposition is pending or can be lodged.

The compulsory licences referred to in (2) and (3) are granted by the Patent Office. The possibility referred to under (3) has caused criticism because it has been misused in order to obtain a compulsory licence under a basic patent on the basis of a younger patent which only entails an insignificant improvement. In the proposal for the new Patent Act this provision has therefore been changed. Compulsory licences will only be possible in order to exploit a patent for inventions which represent a significant step forward compared to the prior art.

Proceedings

Pursuant to the Patent Act, the courts of The Hague are the competent courts in those patent matters which are not within the jurisdiction of the Patent Office. Many patent infringement cases are dealt with in preliminary relief proceedings (see section **6.9.2**).

The defendant can raise *invalidity* arguments in these proceedings. However, if his arguments are based on the same or comparable 'prior art' as already has been considered by the European or Dutch Patent Office during the application procedure, such arguments will generally fail, except of course if the Patent Office has made a clear mistake. Moreover, a defendant who does not file a nullity suit in due time runs the risk (especially in appeal) that his invalidity arguments will be ignored.

6.4 TRADEMARKS

6.4.1 INTRODUCTION

Since 1 January 1971, trademark law in the Netherlands has been governed by the Uniform Benelux Trademark Act (*Eenvormige Beneluxwet op de Merken*, the BTA). Since that date the Benelux countries have a uniform trademark system.

The Benelux Court (*Benelux Gerechtshof*) hears all matters concerning the interpretation of the BTA in final instance.

The old Trademark Act of 1893, having the principle that first use creates trademark rights, is still of importance for the Netherlands Antilles and Aruba as the present legislation in both countries is in conformity with the old Act.

The BTA covers trademarks, service marks and collective marks. Certain changes are under consideration and may be expected in the near future. The most important change will be the revision of the application procedure before the Benelux Trademark Office. Pursuant to the revision, the Benelux Trademark Office will not only check certain formal requirements (as at present) but also material requirements (such as distinctiveness of the trademark or conflicts with prior rights).

In addition, a few minor changes are proposed to bring the BTA in line with the First EC Directive on the harmonisation of the trademark law of the member states of 21 December 1988 (Official Journal 1989 L40).

6.4.2 SIGNS WHICH CAN BE TRADEMARKS

The BTA contains a very broad definition of 'signs' which can be a trademark. This includes the *shape* of goods or their packaging and in general comprise all signs which can distinguish goods or services. This wide definition has resulted in case law in which for instance one colour or a combination of colours has been recognised as trademark. It has also been accepted in case law that the necessary distinctiveness can be achieved after the registration, for instance by intensive use.

Shapes

With respect to the shape of goods and their packaging (whether two or three dimensional) the BTA gives three exceptions to the possibility of being a trademark:

(1) Shapes which are determined by the nature of the goods. The reason for this exception is to prevent limitations on the use of a form which is indispensable for the manufacture or marketing of a product (eg a light bulb).

(2) Shapes which produce industrial results. This exception prevents an overlap between patent rights and trademark rights and ensures that a trademark right cannot prevent a competitor to use a certain 'shape' for his products which shape is useful for the functioning of such product.

(3) Shapes that influence the 'real value' of products. This excludes shapes which in fact determine the value of the product. In other words: products which the public buys because of their shape, eg a beautifully shaped crystal bowl.

Distinctiveness

The Benelux Court has rendered several decisions regarding the question whether a trademark lacked distinctiveness or (in the sense of art 6 *quinquies* B under 2 of the Treaty of Paris 1883 (as amended)) descriptive. The attitude of the Benelux Court is rather liberal. Only purely discriptive signs cannot serve as a trademark. With respect to the question of whether or not a sign is purely descriptive all circumstances of the case are to be weighed. Such circumstances, however, can be put in two important categories:

(1)   It is important to find out whether the trademark *can* actually distinguish the product or service. This can sometimes be established by a market research report.

(2)   It is important to see whether the trademark *should be allowed* to distinguish the goods. Under this category the question arises whether the competitors of the trademark owner would be hampered in selling their products or services if they cannot use the 'sign' to which the trademark owner claims the exclusive rights.

6.4.3   HOW TO OBTAIN TRADEMARK RIGHTS

A trademark right can be obtained by:

(1)   a Benelux 'filing' (in Dutch 'depot'); or

(2)   an international filing under the Madrid Convention 1891 (as amended).

A condition for registration is that either a search for conflicting registration is done within three months before the filing or a request for such search is made at the same time as the filing. Although the search is compulsory, the outcome is purely informative. It cannot give rise to a refusal of registration. The role of the Benelux Trademark Office is passive. If the formalities are fulfilled, a request for registration will be granted. Even clearly invalid trademarks can be registered!

After registration, the trademark's priority date will be the date of the filing.

As a result of the passive role of the Benelux Trademark Office, the real value of a registration can only be tested in the courts.

Nullity

There are several grounds on which the nullity of the filing of a trademark can be invoked. Nullity can be invoked by the plaintiff but also as a defence in infringement proceedings.

A dinstinction is made between absolute and relative nullity. As a general rule, absolute nullity is the result of the trademark conflicting with rules of public interest. Each interested party and the public prosecutor can invoke these absolute grounds for nullity. Relative nullity occurs when the trademark conflicts with the rights of a third party. Relative nullity can only be invoked by or with the participation of such third party.

Absolute nullity
	Grounds for absolute nullity are:
(1)	the filing of a sign, which pursuant to art 1 is not considered a mark, in particular where it is devoid of any distinctiveness within the meaning of art 6 *quinquies* B sub 2 of the Treaty of Paris;
(2)	the filing of a mark which, in order of priority, ranks after that of a similar collective mark irrespective of the good for which such collective mark was filed;
(3)	the filing of a mark which, regardless of the use being made thereof, is contrary to the morality or public policy in one of the Benelux countries or is prohibited by art 6 *ter* of the Treaty of Paris because it consists of flags or emblems of a country which is a party to the Treaty;
(4)	the filing of a mark made for goods or services in respect of which use of the mark is likely to deceive the public;
(5)	the filing of a mark resembling a collective mark regardless of the goods for which it was filed, to which a right was attached which lapsed in the course of the three years preceding the filing.

Relative nullity
	Relatively void is:
(1)	the filing of a mark which is similar to a mark filed earlier for the same kind of goods or services;
(2)	the filing of a mark resembling an individual mark filed by a third party for similar goods or services and to which a right was attached which, on account of the expiration of the registration, lapsed in the course of the three years prior to the filing unless the said third party gave his consent or there was non-use of the said mark during three years after its registration or during five years after the last use;

(3)   the filing of a mark likely to cause confusion with a well-known mark within the meaning of art 6 *bis* of the Treaty of Paris and owned by a third party who has not given his consent;

(4)   the filing effected in bad faith, including *inter alia*:

(a)   filing effected by a person who knows or has no valid excuse for not knowing that within the preceding three years a third party has, in good faith and in the normal manner, used a similar mark for similar goods or services on Benelux territory, and the said third party has not given his consent;

(b)   filing effected by a person who, as a result of direct relations with a third party, knows that during the preceding three years the said party has, in good faith and in the normal manner, used a similar mark for similar goods or services outside the Benelux territory, unless the said third party has given his consent or such knowledge was obtained only after the person effecting the filing had started to use the mark within the Benelux territory.

The system of grounds for 'relative' nullity shows that certain protection is given to trademarks which have lapsed in order to protect their goodwill, but that it is almost impossible to do something about the piracy of a not 'well known' mark which is used abroad but not yet in the Benelux. Only in the case of a *direct relation* (eg the distributor who registers the trademark of his principal) there is a possibility to take action. Foreign companies which are planning to market their products in the future (within three years) in the Benelux should therefore register their trademarks in the Benelux.

6.4.4   LAPSE OF THE TRADEMARK RIGHT

Void registration must be distinguished from the lapse of a trademark right. The declaration of nullity of a registration results in the right being considered not to have existed at all. The lapse of a trademark right does not have retro-active effect. The validity of the right before it lapsed is not affected.

Grounds

Lapse of the trademark right can result from:

(1)   voluntary cancellation of the Benelux filing;

(2)   expiration of the period of validity of the Benelux filing.
       This period is ten years. If the registration is not renewed
       every ten years, the right lapses. The renewal has to be
       requested in a special form against payment of a fee;

(3)   cancellation of an international filing in accordance with the
       rules of the Madrid Convention;

(4)   expiration of an international filing. The period of validity
       of an international filing is 20 years. To prevent losing the
       trademark right, the filing has to be renewed every 20 years;

(5)   voluntary termination of the protection of the international
       filing in the Benelux. The cancellation cannot take place for a
       part of the Benelux. In connection with the Madrid
       Convention the Benelux is seen as one country;

(6)   loss of legal protection in the country of origin of the
       trademark on which the international registration is based.
       The international registration only depends on the protec-
       tion in the country of origin for the creation of the
       international registration and during the first five years of its
       existence. This period of five years is extended if action is
       being taken in the country of origin during the five years
       which leads to loss of protection after the five years have
       passed;

(7)   non-use. If the trademark has, without a valid reason, not
       been used in a normal way within three years following the
       filing or during an uninterrupted period of five years by the
       holder of the trademark or his licensee, the right lapses.
       Symbolical use, such as sale of tokens, is not enough to
       prevent the lapse. What constitutes normal use depends
       very much on the goods. For aeroplanes, advertisements in
       international magazines which also appear in the Nether-
       lands may be sufficient. For cigarettes the sale of thousands
       of packets may not be enough. A valid reason for non-use
       must lay beyond normal entrepreneur's risks;

(8)   the validly acquired trademark becomes generic because of
       the trademark holder's own doing. This may not only occur
       by a certain activity but also by a certain passivity of the
       trademark holder, for example if the holder does not take
       action when the public or his competitor uses his trademark
       in a generic way.

The Benelux Trademark Office plays a passive role in this matter as well. As a result, the loss of a trademark right sometimes appears clearly from the registers (in the case of cancellation or non-renewal) and sometimes it does not.

In the events referred to in (7) and (8), loss as a result of non-use or the trademark becoming a generic name for the goods, the loss of the right can be invoked by each party concerned. If the Court declares that the right has lapsed, it automatically orders the cancellation of the filing to be carried out by the Benelux Trademark Office.

6.4.5 RIGHTS CONFERRED BY THE TRADEMARK

Article 13A BTA distinguishes two categories of acts which can be prohibited by the trademark owner:
(1) The trademark owner can prevent the use of its trademark or a similar sign for the same or similar goods or services (art 13(A) under (1)).
(2) The trademark owner can prevent the use of his trademark or a similar sign in an economic context without a valid reason which use takes place under such circumstances that it may cause damage to the trademark owner (art 13(A) under (2)).

The first category covers the use by an infringer of the trademark or a similar sign for the purpose of distinguishing products or services traded by him from other identical or similar products or services. In that case the protection is absolute. It is not necessary to prove that such use causes damage.

The second category covers all other uses in an economic context. For instance, the use of a trademark or a similar sign for ornamental reasons or for dissimilar goods or services.

6.4.6 'SIMILAR SIGN'

The Benelux Court (in its Union decision 1983) has given the following interpretation to 'similar signs'. There is similarity between a trademark and sign:

> if—taking into consideration all the circumstances of the case and particularly the distinctiveness of the trademark—the trademark and sign, each considered in their entirety and in their relation to each other, have such a similarity,

auditively, visually or conceptually, that as a result there is a possibility that a person who will come across the sign will associate this with the trademark.

With respect to the question of whether or not a sign is infringing the trademark right the following guidelines therefore apply:

(1)   One has to compare the trademark *as registered* with the conflicting sign *as used*. However, circumstances in which the trademark and the conflicting sign are used can be taken in consideration. If a black and white registration is always used on specific packaging or in specific colours, the fact that the conflicting sign is used on packaging with the same shape or in the same colours is a circumstance which has to be taken in consideration when answering the question if 'association' can be caused.

(2)   A further guideline is that the trademark and the conflicting sign should be considered in their totality, therefore including *non-distinctive elements*. This does not exclude the possibility that the similarity between certain parts of the trademark and the sign can have more importance than other parts.

It follows from the Union decision that the distinctiveness of the trademark plays a very important role. Therefore, a famous trademark will have a broader scope of protection than a less famous one. A trademark that lacked distinctiveness when it was registered, can obtain (more) distinctiveness, and therefore (more) protection, by intensive use, advertising etc.

6.4.7   SIMILAR GOODS AND SERVICES

The BTA is not entirely clear as to which criterion has to be applied in order to determine whether goods and/or services are similar. It is clear from the BTA that the administrative classification does not play a role in determining if goods or services are similar. In general, case law shows a tendency to accept rather quickly that there is similarity.

6.4.8   VALID REASON

As explained above in section **6.4.5**, the alleged infringer may invoke a 'valid reason' for his use of the trademark. He could do so when his use of the trademark or the similar sign is not within the scope of the first category of infringement (art 13(A) under (1)) but within the second category (art 13(A) under (2)). In its Klarein decision of 1975 the Benelux Court has given a very restrictive interpretation of a 'valid reason'. In general, to invoke successfully a 'valid reason', the alleged infringer needs to have such need to use precisely that mark or sign that he cannot reasonably be required to refrain from its use even if this may cause damage to the trademark owner. If the alleged infringer has an independent right to use the trademark or similar sign, the right of the trademark owner will be weighed against the right of the alleged infringer. Older rights (eg an older tradename) will in general prevail; younger rights will generally not.

6.4.9   EXHAUSTION

If a product bearing a trademark has been put on the market with the consent of the trademark owner, the trademark owner can no longer invoke his trademark rights unless the condition of the product has been changed. Contrary to patent law, Benelux trademark law has adopted the principle of *international* exhaustion. Therefore, parallel imports—also from countries *outside* the EC—cannot be prevented. It is an unresolved question as to whether this is also the case if the trademark rights are owned by different but related legal entities. Case law of the lower courts indicates that in that case it is still possible to prevent parallel imports. Of course, within the European Community the principle of free circulation of goods prevails and parallel imports cannot be stopped.

6.4.10   COLLECTIVE TRADEMARKS

Collective trademarks have a different function from individual trademarks. They are meant to indicate a certain quality of the goods or services. Because of this 'guarantee function', special additional rules are set out in Chapter II of the BTA for the purpose of protecting the public interest.

A trademark is collective if this is stated in the registration and if it serves as an indicator of common characteristics of goods, originating from different companies which put the mark on the goods under the supervision of the collective trademark holder.

For a valid registration of the collective trademark, 'regulations' on the use and supervision must have been registered. The holder of the collective trademark is *not* entitled to use the trademark for his own products.

Scope of protection

The protection of the collective trademark is very broad. The holder of a collective trademark can oppose each use that is being made of the mark or a similar sign irrespective of the goods for which it is used. There is no 'valid reason' exception to this rule. The only exception is that the holder of a collective trademark cannot oppose the use of a prior registered individual trademark. Unless the regulations state otherwise, a lawsuit to obtain an injunction or to claim damages can only be initiated by the holder of the collective trademark. The users of the collective mark are not allowed to take action on their own. If explicitly stipulated, the holder of the collective trademark can claim monetary damages incurred by the users.

Nullity or lapse

The grounds for nullity of the filing of a collective trademark are extended by nullity because of invalid 'regulations'. In addition to the rules set for the lapse of individual trademarks, the collective trademark right will also lapse if the holder of the right uses the mark himself or if he permits or tolerates the use of the mark against the regulations.

6.4.11   CONCLUSION—FUTURE DEVELOPMENTS

The BTA is a modern trademark Act which recognises, in addition to the function of 'origin', the other modern functions of the trademark, particularly the 'goodwill function'. It protects the trademark against each infringement of this function.

Under the influence of the BTA, the first EC Directive on the harmonisation of trademark laws (see section **6.4.1**) contains the 'association' criterion (in other words there is a trademark infringement in case of possible association between the infringing sign and the trademark) and a provision which makes it possible to act against the use of a trademark for dissimilar goods and service. The BTA will only need minor changes to comply with the Directive.

6.5 DESIGN LAW

6.5.1 INTRODUCTION

Dutch law does not provide for a special regime protecting *industrial* designs. A proposal for such regime has been suspended by the Dutch government after the introduction of plans for a new Patent Act which provides among others for a short term registration patent (see section **6.3.1**).

As of 1 January 1975, *ornamental* designs can be protected under the Uniform Benelux Design Act (*Eenvormige Beneluxwet inzake Tekeningen of Modellen*) which provides protection by registration for the whole territory of the Benelux. The provisions of the Act apply to the whole of the Benelux thus providing one uniform design system for the Benelux countries. The Benelux Court deals with questions of interpretation of the Act in final instance.

6.5.2 TREATIES

The Benelux is a party to the Treaty of The Hague 1925 (as amended) which enables Dutch citizens, residents and companies to file an international registration covering the countries which are party to the Treaty.

6.5.3 SCOPE OF PROTECTION

Under the Uniform Benelux Design Act protection can be obtained for the new appearance ('get-up') of an article of use (*gebruiksvoorwerp*) as far as such appearance is not necessary for a technical effect of the article. No protection can be claimed for designs or features of designs which are necessary to give the design its function of use.

A further requirement for obtaining protection is that the design is *new*. 'New' is defined in the Act as follows: the design, or a design which only shows minor differences with the design, has not been known in the Benelux in 'the relevant circles of trade or industry' during a period of 50 years preceding the filing of the design.

The meaning of 'minor differences' will be discussed below in section **6.5.7**. Contrary to the Patent Act, the Uniform Benelux Design Act basically contains the principle of *national novelty*. However, it is quite possible that the exhibition of a design on a trade exhibition in Germany takes away the novelty of the design in the Benelux. This will be the case if such an exhibition is visited by persons working in the relevant circles of trade or industry in the Benelux.

The Uniform Benelux Design Act does not know any requirement with respect to aesthetic value. 'Novelty' as described above is the only criterion.

6.5.4 THE REGISTRATION

In order to obtain protection it is necessary to make an international filing or to file with the Benelux Design Office. Because of the 'novelty' requirement, such filing has to be carried out before the product is put on the market. This timely filing is—as under the Patent Act—essential because the designer cannot rely on the general rules of unfair competition in order to prevent—even slavish—copying of his designs if there was the possibility of design protection and no application had been made.

The Benelux Design Office only checks the filing for formal requirements. There is no examination with respect to material requirements such as 'novelty'. The design is registered in the Design Register as soon as possible. The design is dated and in force as of the date of the filing with the Benelux Design Office. As the Benelux Design Office only ensures that formal requirements have been complied with, the ultimate decision as to whether or not the registration confers valid rights will be made by the courts. In general, the design is published as soon as possible in the Journal for Benelux designs or models (*Recueil des Dessins ou Modèles Benelux*). The registration expires after five years but can be renewed for two further periods of five years.

6.5.5 INVALIDITY

Any interested party, including the public prosecutor, can invoke the nullity of a design registration on the following grounds:

(1)   lack of novelty;
(2)   the design is contrary to public policy or good morals;
(3)   from the publication the essential features of the design do
       not become sufficiently clear.
       The nullity has retro-active effect.

6.5.6   ENTITLEMENT TO THE DESIGN

In principle, the first applicant is entitled to the design.
However, the following exceptions apply to this rule:
(1)   The actual designer. The person who actually made the
       design and did not agree to the filing has the right to claim the
       registration in his name or the nullity of the filing. The
       possibility of claiming the registration lapses five years after
       the filing.
(2)   The employer or commissioner of the design. Designs made
       by employees in the performance of their job or made on
       order for the use in trade or industry will normally belong to
       the employer or the person who commissioned the work.

6.5.7   THE PROTECTION AFFORDED BY A REGISTRATION

In general, the holder of the registered design may prohibit
all commercial acts involving:
(1)   his design; or
(2)   a design which shows only minor differences to his design.

This criterion referred to in (2) means that the scope of
protection conferred by a design is very limited and more so than
for instance under copyright or trademark law. In general, one
can say that there will be an infringement if the relevant public
(the potential customers for the product embodying the design)
might confuse the designs. In other words, if the relevant public
coming across the allegedly infringing design could think that it is
looking at the registered design.

6.5.8   PRIOR USE

The person who had already made, or had started making,
the same design prior to the filing, cannot infringe the design
rights resulting from the (subsequent) registration. This provision is the same as the provision under the Dutch Patent Act.

6.5.9   OVERLAP WITH OTHER INTELLECTUAL PROPERTY RIGHTS

As already indicated it is not possible to invoke the general rules of unfair competition in order to protect a design that qualifies for protection under the Uniform Benelux Design Act.

Copyright

The Act contains specific provisions with respect to copyright. Under the Dutch Copyright Act, designs can be protected if they are 'original', which generally is interpreted as meaning that they should show the 'personal mark' of the designer. Such 'personal mark' is generally considered to be present if it is unlikely that the same design could have been created independently by another designer.

The Uniform Benelux Design Act provides that designs can be protected by copyright if they have a 'clear artistic nature'. The Benelux Court has decided that this criterion is not different from the criterion used under the Dutch Copyright Act. This means that the Uniform Benelux Design Act does *not* limit the number of designs which enjoy copyright protection.

Trademark

Further concurrence is possible with the Uniform Benelux Trademark Act. It is possible (assuming the design is distinguishing the goods or services of the trademark owner) that a design can also be the subject of trademark protection. Such concurrence is only possible to a limited extent because the Uniform Benelux Trademark Act excludes from protection two or three-dimensional 'shapes' (*vormen*) which influence the 'essential value' of the product. Therefore, if the aesthetical value of the design determines to an important degree its market value, no trademark protection is possible.

6.6   TRADENAME

6.6.1   INTRODUCTION

Tradename law is set out in the Tradename Act (*Handelsnaamwet*). The Act contains rules which can protect the public against tradenames giving an incorrect impression about the entreprise or its owners. The Act also contains provisions which make it possible to act against tradenames which are 'confusingly similar' to other tradenames or to trademarks.

6.6.2 DEFINITION

The Act defines a tradename as 'the name under which an enterprise is acting'. It is accepted that an enterprise may have and often has more than one tradename.

'Enterprise' has been interpreted by the courts in a broad sense and can include foundations, accountancy firms etc. The Act deals with names only. For protection of corporate logo etc (if not also a trademark), one has to rely on the general rules of unfair competition.

6.6.3 REQUIREMENTS

Unlike a trademark, a tradename does not have to be 'distinctive'. However, if a tradename lacks distinctiveness, the protection against conflicting tradenames will be very limited as it is unlikely that non-identical tradenames will be confused with such an undistinctive tradename.

It is prohibited to use a tradename which misleads the public about the ownership of the enterprise. Furthermore it is forbidden to use a tradename which gives a wrong suggestion with respect to the legal entity to which the enterprise belongs or with respect to the nature and significance of the enterprise.

6.6.4 HOW TO OBTAIN TRADENAME RIGHTS

The protection afforded by the Tradename Act comes into existence by the *use* of the name for an enterprise in the Netherlands.

Tradenames of foreign enterprises cannot be used in the Netherlands by another enterprise if they are known within the Netherlands.

The tradename is attached to the enterprise and the rights cannot be transferred without the enterprise. It is therefore not possible to buy and transfer a tradename as such without also acquiring certain assets which are essential for the activities being carried out under the tradename.

6.6.5   PROTECTION OF THE TRADENAME

Article 5 of the Act protects the older tradename against a younger tradename which is so similar that it may be feared that the public will get confused between the two enterprises using the similar tradenames, taking into consideration the nature and the location of the enterprises concerned.

Article 5A contains a similar provision with respect to an older trade*mark* and a younger tradename. However, in such a situation the trademark owner will in general rely on art 13A(2) of the Benelux Trademark Act because that provision is not limited to protection against the danger of confusion but protects the trademark owner against each use without 'valid reason' which may cause damages.

There is no provision in the Act which deals with the older tradename and the *younger mark*. However, in case of a possibility of confusion, the tradename owner can rely on the general rules of unfair competition.

The general rules of unfair competition also protect the tradename against certain acts detrimental to the goodwill attached to such tradename (for instance, dilution of the tradename, eg the use of the tradename Harrods for a petrol station at Maastricht). In such cases possibility of confusion is not a condition for protection.

6.7   COPYRIGHT

6.7.1   INTRODUCTION

Dutch copyright law is set out in the Copyright Act 1912 (*Auteurswet 1912*). Since 1912 the Act has been amended several times.

The Netherlands is a party to the Berne Convention 1886 (as amended) and the Universal Copyright Convention 1967.

The Netherlands provide for strong copyright protection under the influence of a well established pro-copyright lobby. The most recent proof for this can be found in a proposal for a duty to be paid in respect of blank video and audiotapes which is expected to be enacted in the near future.

Furthermore, copyright provides protection for a wide

range of works from computer programs to industrial designs. In general, the courts tend not to require a high degree of originality for protection which, combined with the absence of any formal requirement such as registration, also makes copyright a strong weapon against competitors.

6.7.2 WHAT CAN BE PROTECTED

Original works

The Act states that copyright exists with respect to 'works of literature, science and art'. The Act gives a non-limitative list of examples of 'works'.

In principle—see for certain exceptions below—all '*original*' works are protected. Original means that the work needs to have the 'personal stamp' of the maker. In other words, it should be impossible that an identical work could independently be made. It is clear that the nature of the 'work' often defines the possibility of orginality. Therefore, it will certainly be possible to claim originality with respect to a list of data. However, the actual originality will then have to be found in the way such listing is presented. This will be more difficult than originality with respect to a novel.

Expression

In order to be protected it is necessary that the work has been 'expressed' in a certain specific way. This can be a written form (a book) or an oral form (a lecture) or any other form. It excludes protection of ideas, styles and methods (eg the idea to use birds as a decoration for tiles) as such. The Copyright Act mentions, *inter alia*, the following examples of works: books, leaflets, newspapers and all other written material.

Protection of non-original material

A unique feature of Dutch copyright law is that all written material is protected, even when it is not original. If written material is not original it is only protected if it can be proven that it has been *copied* and is (or is meant to be) made public. This provision of Dutch copyright law can be of great help against the copying of software as it makes a discussion with respect to the originality of the copied work unnecessary.

Works

In addition to written material, the Act mentions many other examples of 'works', which can also be found in the Berne Convention.

Since 1985 the Act has included as a special category film works.

The last category reads 'works of applied art and designs and models of industry'. In this category products that are the result of industrial design can be protected. Case law gives many examples: furniture, fashion designs, home appliances, games (not the idea of the game itself, but the form which has been given to such idea).

The word 'art' which is mentioned in the last category does not have a special meaning. For this category it is also sufficient that a work has a minimum of 'originality'. It should be noted that these works, if first published in another Berne Convention country, only enjoy protection in the Netherlands if they are also protected in their own country.

Computer programs

Computer programs have been proposed as a separate category of 'works' but this proposal has been withdrawn as the proposal also envisaged making clear that computer programs could not be protected under the category 'written material'.

As we have discussed above, this would have meant that no protection could be obtained against the copying of non-original computer programs. Critics stated that this would in fact mean a decrease in the possibilities of protection of computer programs. Although there is no decision of the Supreme Court on this point, it is quite certain that original computer programs are protected under the Copyright Act whether or not they are considered 'written material'.

This is the case with system software and application software. The result of working with a computer (computer generated works) may also be protected if sufficiently original. Furthermore, the specific way the results are presented on the screen may also be protected.

The Court of Appeal at Amsterdam (overruling a lower court's decision) has granted copyright protection to a videogame.

6.7.3   ENTITLEMENT TO COPYRIGHT

Maker(s)

The person who makes a work is entitled to the copyright. This general principle has a few important exceptions. The person who claims copyright will have to prove that, but if the work carries his name than he is presumed to be the maker unless it is proven that this presumption is incorrect.

Very often the efforts of various people result in a certain product. If the work of the different persons can be distinguished (eg song and music), each person has copyright with respect to his own work. If the work cannot be divided, the parties jointly enjoy one copyright with respect to the result of their efforts.

A person who puts together different works by different persons may enjoy a copyright of his own in the compilation. The authors of such different works of course keep their copyrights with respect to their own work.

Film rights

Since 1985 the Act has contained specific provisions with respect to film rights. These new provisions are only applicable for films the production of which started after 1 August 1985. The producer (the person who is financially responsible for the making and distribution of the film) automatically obtains all copyrights necessary for the exploitation of the film unless a copyright owner (eg the writer of the script) has reserved his rights in writing. Composers and text writers of film music are excepted from this automatic transfer of copyright.

Further exceptions

Two further exceptions to the rule that the maker of a work obtains the copyright are the following.

First, the employer is entitled to the copyright in work made by an employee if the employment consists of the making of such works.

Secondly, if a work is made public as originating from a company, foundation or another legal entity, such legal entity will be considered to have the copyright unless the name of the true maker is mentioned in the work or parties have agreed otherwise. Therefore, the copyright(s) in an advertising campaign will probably belong to the company for which the advertisement is made and not to the advertising agency which created the campaign.

6.7.4   WHAT IS NOT PROTECTED

Ideas

We have already stated that ideas, styles, methods etc cannot be protected, as in order to obtain protection it is necessary that the creation has been expressed in a specific form.

Performers' rights

Furthermore, there is no protection under the Act for performing artists, broadcasting programs and record producers. However, in the near future the Netherlands will ratify the Rome Convention 1961 and the Geneva Convention 1971 and pass an Act which will provide for protection. Under the present law, performers' rights are protected under the rules of unfair competition (see section **6.2.2**).

Further exceptions

There is no copyright with respect to the text of Acts, regulations or judgements. The Supreme Court has furthermore ruled that it is not an act of unfair competition to publish a photocopy of the text of a regulation.

6.7.5   RIGHTS OF THE COPYRIGHT OWNER

Multiplying

The Act states that the owner of the copyright has the exclusive right to *make public and multiply* his work. The Act gives a very broad interpretation of these acts. With respect to multiplying, the Act makes clear that this is not restricted to slavish copying. Translations or films made of a book are also multiplications.

The scope of protection is rather broad. With respect to infringement, however, the nature of the work to be protected will play a significant role. In general one could say the more original the work, the more protection it enjoys.

Publication

The Act distinguishes between primary and secondary publication. If a record is put on the market by the copyright owner, the rights with respect to such primary publication are exhausted. However, the copyright owner can still prevent the playing of the record *in public* (eg on the radio or in a discotheque). 'Public' is in fact everything except playing—without asking payment—for family, friends and comparable gatherings.

The Supreme Court has—not surprisingly—decided that the renting-out of records which have been put on the market by the copyright owner is allowed because the primary copyright is exhausted.

At present, new legislation is pending which would give the copyright owner the right to reasonable compensation in case of the renting-out of his work.

With respect to secondary publication, the Supreme Court has decided that the transmission by a cable network of a television programme which is broadcast at the same time is an infringement of the copyright with respect to the work which is broadcast, even if the receivers of the cable signal can also receive the television programme directly by air. This is only different if the broadcaster also exploits the cable network.

6.7.6 LIMITATIONS ON COPYRIGHT

The copyright expires in general *50 years* after the year in which the maker died. In certain other cases, for instance if the maker (eg an employer) is a company, the copyright expires 50 years after the year of publication. Works which have first been published in another country will enjoy the same length of copyright protection in the Netherlands as in the country where it was first published, but in no event longer than the protection the work would have enjoyed if it had first been published in the Netherlands.

6.7.7 MORAL RIGHTS

In addition to the right to multiply his work and make his work public the copyright owner also has certain moral rights which are personal and cannot be transferred.

Moral rights continue to exist after the primary publication rights have been exhausted (eg after a painting has been put on the market).

The moral rights are the following. The maker can prevent:

(1)   publication of the work without mentioning the name of the maker unless this would be unreasonable;
(2)   publication under a different name or title;
(3)   changes to the work unless this would be unreasonable;
(4)   deformation, mutilation or other impairment of the work.

In addition the maker always has the right to make certain changes in his work even after he has assigned his copyright.

The question of whether or not a work can be destroyed is judged on the basis of the question of whether such destruction is an 'impairment of the work'.

6.7.8   PERMITTED USE OF COPYRIGHT BY THIRD PARTIES

Use of the copyright by third parties is allowed for the following reasons:
(1)   News and other messages can be freely copied. Articles or radio and television programmes with respect to current economic, political and religious subjects can only be copied if no reservation of copyright has been made. If necessary for the reporting of a current event, photographs, film, radio or television may show a work protected by copyright for a short time.
(2)   Citation of the work in another work by a third party. Citation has to take place in the context of another work (eg in a book review) and the extent has to be reasonable.
(3)   Educational purposes. Copying is allowed but the copyright owner has to be paid a reasonable indemnification.
(4)   Own use. For own use one is entitled to make a few copies of a work protected by copyright. However, this right of the own user has several exceptions. For instance, copying a complete book, magazine etc is not allowed as long as these can be bought. Government institutions, libraries, schools and universities are allowed to make copies for use in the carrying out of their work. However, they have to pay compensation for such use. Companies have the same right for use by their employees with respect to scientific articles and small excerpts from scientific books.
(5)   Portrait. A person can always object to the publication of his picture which has been made with his approval. He himself has the right to make copies but he does not have the right to

publish his picture. A person whose picture is made without his approval can object to publication if he has a reasonable interest in doing so.

(6) Public authorities. Publications by or on behalf of public authorities can be copied and published freely unless copyright has been reserved.

(7) Public roads. Works of architecture and art which are permanently placed along a public road can be copied if the copy is clearly different from the original (eg a postcard) and the work is not the most important part of the copy.

(8) Broadcasting. The Act furthermore provides for the possiblity of a compulsory licence for the use of works by broadcasting organisations.

6.7.9 ENFORCEMENT OF COPYRIGHT

The Act contains special provisions with respect to enforcement. Products which infringe upon a copyright can be seized and the copyright owner can demand that the infringing products will be handed to him (in such cases the court can ask the copyright owner to pay certain compensation) or will be destroyed. The copyright owner can ask for damages and for payment by the infringer of all profits which have been realised as a result of the infringement.

6.8 KNOW-HOW

Dutch law does not recognise an exclusive title with respect to know-how, trade secrets and/or technical information (hereinafter referred to collectively as 'know-how'). In general, it is therefore not possible to prevent third parties from using knowhow even if such know-how has become known to such party by breach of a contractual or statutory obligation not to disclose such know-how. Only if this third party has provoked disclosure by another person would it be possible to act against such third party on the basis of tort.

The only protection of know-how in the Netherlands—and therefore its value—lies in the fact that other persons do not (yet) know what the person who has the know-how knows and such knowledge has a certain value. If the owner of the know-how wants to exploit the know-how by, for example, licensing, he is only protected by contract. Without an explicit (or implied) contract, there is no obligation to keep know-how secret.

The Dutch Criminal Code helps the owner of know-how in two ways with the protection of this know-how. First of all it contains a provision which prohibits the breach of a legal obligation to confidentiality. This provision is not only relevant for lawyers and other professionals but also for civil servants who obtain information from companies in the exercise of their duties. Generally, such civil servants have a legal obligation to keep the knowledge obtained in the performance of their duty confidential.

The second provision in the Criminal Code is more important because it penalises employees who do not keep secrets; only, however, in as far as such employees were *bound* to secrecy. It is therefore important for an employer to have clear secrecy directives for its employees, preferably in the employment agreement.

6.9 INTERNATIONAL ASPECTS AND LITIGATION

6.9.1 INTERNATIONAL ASPECTS OF UNFAIR COMPETITION

Introduction

Because the Netherlands is a small country, the economy of which is largely dependent on international trade, it is not surpising that very often unfair competition cases have international aspects. We will make a few remarks about the applicable law in such cases and about jurisdiction.

Applicable law

Nowadays the generally accepted principle is that in international cases a Dutch court will apply the law of the market on which the competition, subject of the litigation, takes place. This will even be the case if a Dutch plaintiff and a Dutch defendant have a dispute with respect to alleged unfair competition in, for instance, Germany. In such a case a Dutch court will apply German law.

In preliminary relief proceedings in particular, the president of the District Court will assume that the unfair competition rules of another country are the same as in the Netherlands (especially in countries which are members of the Treaty of Paris). In such cases it is up to the defendant to prove that the law of the country concerned is different and that what would be considered unfair competition in the Netherlands is not unfair competition in such other countries.

Jurisdiction

If an act of unfair competition takes place in the whole of the Netherlands, the plaintiff has the possibility to choose any one of the presidents of the 19 District Courts in order to obtain an injunction.

This possibility does not exist in patent cases as the courts of the Hague have exclusive jurisdiction in such matters.

It is clear that a possibility of choice leads to 'forum shopping'.

If the defendant is established in the Netherlands the court of the defendant's residence will also have jurisdiction and will be able to give decisions which have effect outside the Netherlands. It is, for instance, possible to obtain an injunction against trademark infringement in another country. This is also the case if the plaintiff is established in the Netherlands and the defendant outside the Netherlands as far as the defendant is not residing in a country which is party to the European Convention on Jurisdiction and Enforceability of Decisions in Civil and Commercial Matters 1968. A Dutch plaintiff can therefore obtain a decision against a Taiwanese company forbidding, for instance, the Taiwanese company infringing Italian design rights belonging to the Dutch plaintiff.

There are several other possibilities to establish jurisdiction of Dutch courts.

It follows that the Netherlands is an attractive country for international forum shopping. In many cases it is possible to obtain a quick result in preliminary relief proceedings. Such proceedings are relatively cheap and very informal while the judges are generally highly competent.

6.9.2   LITIGATION IN UNFAIR COMPETITION MATTERS

Preliminary relief

Many unfair competition cases are dealt with in preliminary relief proceedings (see **Introduction**) because they are considered urgent which is the requirement for such proceedings.

Preliminary relief proceedings start with the president of the District Court giving a date for a hearing. In really urgent matters this can be a matter of hours but normally such date will be set for a few weeks later. The plaintiff has to issue a writ of summons in which he states the grounds for, and the contents of, his claims. On the date set by the president both parties will give their arguments orally. Proof is normally supplied by way of affidavits and exhibits. The president can hear witnesses or ask questions of the parties. The whole procedure is rather informal. The judgement is immediately enforceable and non-compliance with the judgement results in the forfeiture of penalty sums to be paid to the plaintiff.

Court orders

The president is in fact free to impose any measure which he deems necessary. In competition cases this will generally be an injunction forbidding continuation of the infringing use, an order to take back infringing products already delivered and the handing over of a list with names and adresses of customers in order to enable the plaintiff to check whether the products have been taken back.

It is also possible to ask for an advance of the amount of damages. Such an advance may particularly be granted in copyright cases.

The president may also order the defendant to write rectification letters or place advertisements in which the judgement of the president is mentioned.

Appeal and normal proceedings

Appeal and 'cassation' of judgements in preliminary relief proceedings are available. The plaintiff who has enforced a decision which is overturned in appeal (or in the 'normal' proceedings) has to compensate the defendant for the damages caused by the enforcement of the decision.

Preliminary relief proceedings can always be followed by 'normal' proceedings which will lead to a *definite* decision. Invalidity arguments can be raised as a defence in preliminary relief proceedings but normal proceedings are necessary in order to declare the invalidity of intellectual property rights.

Normal proceedings will start with a writ of summons,

followed by a written statement of answer and (most of the time) statements of reply and of rejoinder. Subsequently, oral arguments are usually delivered. The court can give an interlocutory decision, ordering a party to prove certain facts or ordering expert advice.

It is always possible to file (eg for invalidity) a cross complaint.

Appeal (and cassation) can be instituted against the judgment in 'normal' proceedings.

Discovery

Dutch law does have a system of 'discovery' such as exists in the UK. However, it is possible to request a *preliminary* hearing of witnesses. Such a hearing will take place before a judge and gives the prospective claimant the opportunity to obtain information about the (prospective) defendant and to establish certain facts.

Attachment

As a security for monetary damages it is possible to seize goods of the defendant or monies owed to the defendant by a third party.

Only in copyright cases is it possible to seize infringing products. In other cases this is not possible, but the same result can be obtained by seizing such products as security for monetary damages.

Other procedures

The Netherlands has implemented EC Regulation No 3842/ 86 which establishes measures to prevent the bringing into circulation of counterfeit products. However, these measures (which require the cooperation of the customs authorities) are in practice less effective than private action. Despite the fact that infringement of intellectual property rights and counterfeiting in general are often criminal offences, normally (but there are exceptions) the public prosecutor is not very willing to act except in very serious cases.

7

COMMERCIAL CONTRACTS

7.1 INTRODUCTION

7.1.1 NEW LAW

As of 1 January 1992 the general law of contract can be found in Book 6 of the (new) Dutch Civil Code. Certain specific contracts (such as the contract for the sale and purchase of goods) are provided for in Book 7. Only four parts of Book 7 came into force on 1 January 1992, together with Books 3, 5 and 6.

Book 8, relating to transport (sea and land), came into force on 1 April 1991.

7.1.2 PRE-CONTRACTUAL RELATIONS

The Civil Code does not contain provisions with respect to the pre-contractual phase. However, in case law the rule has developed that parties who start to negotiate must behave in a way so as to take into consideration each other's justified interests. In general, three phases can be distinguished in the negotiating process:

(1) the initial phase: the parties may withdraw without consequences;

(2) the middle phase: a party may only withdraw if he pays the costs incurred by the other party;

(3) the final phase: in view of the circumstances the parties may believe that a certain contract will be concluded. In such a situation a withdrawing party may be confronted with an order to continue the negotiations or to pay full damages (costs and lost profits) to the other party. It is therefore advisable to agree at an early stage (for instance in a letter of intent) on the consequences of one party withdrawing in a

later stage or of the parties concluding that no agreement can be reached.

7.1.3   FREEDOM OF THE PARTIES

The basic principle of the law of contract is that parties are free to conclude any type of agreement irrespective of whether such an agreement is specifically provided for in statutory law.

This freedom is restricted by public law, by public order and good morals. An example of such a restriction: a clause in an agreement which is contrary to art 85, para 1 of the EC Treaty is null and void on the basis of art 85, para 2. Under Dutch law, such partial nullity will not lead to nullity of the whole agreement, unless—in view of the contents and the purpose of the agreement—there is an unbreakable relation between the part which is null and void and the remainder of the agreement.

The freedom of the parties is further restricted by mandatory law which very often protects the weaker party (such as the employee, the tenant, the consumer). Such mandatory law automatically forms part of the agreement to which it applies. Clauses which are contrary to mandatory law are void.

Finally, the freedom of the parties is limited in that reasonableness and fairness may under certain circumstances render certain agreed rights unenforceable or create contractual rights in areas not covered by the parties in their agreement.

7.1.4   FORMALITIES

In general, agreements can be concluded without formalities. However, there are many exceptions to this rule for reasons of legal certainty or protection of the weaker party. For instance, hire-purchase agreements and certain clauses in employment agreements will only be valid when made in writing (see also for employment agreements section **2.3**). The agreement for the purchase and sale of real property does not require any formality to be complied with. In Dutch practice the somewhat misleading term 'preliminary purchase agreement' (*voorlopig koopcontract*) is often used for such an agreement. However, such 'preliminary purchase agreement' is not preliminary, but final and binding and obliges the seller to transfer the property (by notarial deed) and the buyer to pay the purchase price.

7.1.5 INTERPRETATION OF AGREEMENTS

The interpretation of agreements tends to be less literal and more purpose orientated than in the common law legal systems. An important feature of the Dutch law of contract is the principle of 'good faith' (*goede trouw*). The New Civil Code will introduce a new but similar concept of 'reasonableness and fairness' (*redelijkheid en billijkheid*). Reasonableness and fairness may supplement and also replace contractual obligations. See also section **7.1.3**.

7.2 INTERNATIONAL CONTRACTS

7.2.1 INTERNATIONAL ASPECTS

If an agreement does not exclusively fall within the Dutch legal sphere, but also touches upon the legal sphere of another country the question arises which law is applicable.

7.2.2 FREEDOM OF CHOICE

In this international context Dutch law recognises the freedom of the parties to choose the law governing their agreement. A choice of foreign law in principle also excludes the applicability of mandatory provisions of Dutch law except if these provisions protect such important Dutch interests that they should not be set aside (see section **7.2.4**). A choice of law can be express but also implied as long as it is not doubtful that the parties had the intention to make such choice. The parties may also choose the applicable law after they have entered into the agreement.

7.2.3 TREATIES ON APPLICABLE LAW

EC Convention

The EC Convention on the law applicable to contractual obligations of 19 June 1980, which came into force on 1 September 1991 for the Netherlands, not only confirms the freedom of the parties to choose the applicable law but also provides which law is applicable in the absence of choice. The provisions of the Convention apply in all international situations involving the laws of different countries irrespective of whether application of the convention would lead to the applicability of the laws of a non-treaty country.

Other treaties

Because Dutch private international law is not codified, Dutch courts tend to follow the rules set out in treaties drafted by the the Hague Conference, even if such treaties are not (yet) in force in the Netherlands.

The Netherlands is party to treaties which give provisions of uniform law for certain specific contracts such as the the Hague Convention relating to a uniform law on the international sale of goods of 1 July 1964 and the the Hague Convention relating to a uniform law on the formation of contracts for the international sale of goods of the same date.

On 1 January 1992 the (United Nations) Convention on Contracts for the International Sale of Goods of 11 April 1980 came into force for the Netherlands and replace these the Hague Conventions.

7.2.4 MANDATORY LAW OF AN EXCEPTIONAL NATURE

Notwithstanding the fact that a certain law governs an agreement, it remains possible under Dutch private international law that another system of law will prevail. This would be the case if the compliance with certain of its (mandatory) rules is of such essence to a certain state, that precedence should be given to the application of such rules rather than to the application of the law of choice (see, *inter alia*, the Supreme Court's Alnati decision 1966).

For instance the Dutch rules which grant protection to the tenant will be held applicable to property located in the Netherlands, despite the fact that foreign law governs the tenancy agreement. The same rule has been applied with respect to Dutch regulations relating to currency and prices.

On the other hand, such provisions may not be held applicable to agreements to which Dutch law applies but which have no connection with the Netherlands.

This principle resulted in the Dutch Decree on Labour Relations 1945 which requires a licence for the termination of an employment agreement (see section **2.7.3**) being held applicable in respect of an employee who worked in the Netherlands under an employment agreement governed by foreign law. The same licence was, however, not deemed necessary in the case of an employee who worked outside the Netherlands under an employment agreement governed by Dutch law.

In international cases Dutch courts will also take into consideration mandatory provisions of an exceptional nature of the law of foreign countries if Dutch law or the law of a third country is applicable. Therefore, a Dutch court will apply US antitrust law to an agreement between a Dutch company and a French company involving certain transactions in the US. It will apply such law even if the parties have made a choice for Dutch or French law.

7.3   AGENCY

7.3.1   COMMERCIAL AGENCY AGREEMENT

According to Dutch law a commercial agency agreement exists if the following criteria are met:

(1)   The agent is self employed. If the agent is a natural person and not a legal entity and especially if he represents only one principal, an agent will be considered an employee (and the agreement between agent and principal an employment agreement) if it is clear that there is a relation of authority between principal and agent. Not the wording used in the contract, but the actual relation between the parties is decisive for the qualification as agency or as employment agreement. Qualification as an employment agreement may have serious consequences for the principal who may be held liable to pay taxes and social security premiums;

(2)   The relationship between agent and principal is not of an incidental nature; *and*

(3)   The agent acts as an intermediary in the conclusion of contracts between the principal and third parties or he concludes contracts in the name and for the account of the principal. This means that there will be no contract between the third party and the agent but only between the principal and the third party.

7.3.2 THE RELEVANT PROVISIONS

General

The Commercial Code (art 74 *et seq*) contains detailed provisions for agreements which, on the basis of the criteria set out above, qualify as commercial agency agreements.

In 1989 the provisions in the Commercial Code were slightly changed to bring the provisions in line with the EC Directive on coordination of the law regarding commercial agents (Official Journal No L387/17 of 31 December 1986).

The provisions for commercial agents in the Commercial Code are partly of a supplemental nature and partly of a mandatory nature.

Supplemental provisions

'*Supplemental*' means that if the parties have not provided for situations for which the relevant provisions have been written, they will be binding upon the parties. However, the parties have the right not to adopt these provisions.

Mandatory provisions

A large number of the provisions are of a *mandatory* nature. This means that they automatically become part of the agreement between the parties. The parties do not have the right to agree otherwise. These provisions generally intend to protect the agent. There is no clear-cut case law on the question of whether the mandatory provisions are of such a nature that they will also prevail over a choice of foreign law (see section **7.2.4**).

In general, this would seem less likely if the agent is a legal entity and not a natural person.

The following provisions of the Commercial Code are mandatory for both principal and agent.

Written document

Each party to the agency agreement must provide the other party at its request with a signed document setting out the then existing terms of the agency agreement.

Due care and information

The agent must properly look after its principal's interests and follow his reasonable instructions. The agent must provide all necessary information to the principal, in particular all contracts negotiated or concluded on his behalf.

'Delcredere'

The agent can assume liability for the proper performance by third parties of their contractual obligations *vis-à-vis* the principal. Such liability can only be undertaken in writing. The liability is restricted to the amount of the commission to which the agent is entitled in respect of the relevant contract. If, however, the agent, on behalf of his principal, has himself entered into a contract with a third party, his liability may exceed the amount of the commission but the courts may mitigate the amount of such liability.

Duties of the principal

The principal must do everything to enable the agent to carry out its work. In particular, the principal must provide the agent with the necessary documentation regarding the products and/or services and give him all necessary information.

He must notify the agent immediately when he anticipates that the volume of transactions will be significantly lower than the agent could expect. He must also inform the agent within a reasonable period of his acceptance, refusal or non-performance of a transaction procured by the agent.

Commission after termination

The agent is entitled to a commission with respect to preparatory work for contracts which are concluded after the termination of the agency agreement:

(1) if these contracts are concluded mainly as a result of the agent's actions and within a reasonable period after the termination of the agency agreement; or

(2) if the order of the third party reached the agent or the principal before such termination.

Performance by third party

The principal can stipulate that a commission will only be due if the third party has performed his contractual obligations, provided, however, such stipulation has been explicitly made.

Statement of commissions due and control

The principal is obliged to provide the agent with a monthly written statement of the commissons due, unless the parties agree that such a statement must be provided every two or three months. The agent is entitled to inspect the underlying evidence and to hire an expert for this purpose. The agent must keep the evidence confidential.

Minimum notice period

The notice period must be at least one month for the first year of the agency agreement, two months for the second year and three months for the third and subsequent years. If the parties have agreed on longer notice periods, these may not be shorter for the principal than for the agent.

If an agent is a natural person and does not have more than two principals (see also section **7.3.1**), the agency agreement can only be terminated after having obtained a licence from the Regional Director for Employment Policy (see section **2.7**). Such a licence is not necessary if the agent regularly employs two or more persons. Moreover, no licence is necessary if the agency agreement has been concluded for a fixed term.

However, if after this fixed term the parties continue the agency agreement (whether or not for another fixed term), a licence will be required.

Finally, no licence is necessary if termination takes place for 'urgent reasons' or if the agency agreement is terminated by the court (see below).

Termination for 'urgent reasons'

The party which terminates the agreement
(1)   before the agreed term has expired; or
(2)   without observance of the statutory or agreed notice period; and
(3)   without the consent of the other party,
is liable for damages, unless the termination is based on an 'urgent reason'; the law gives a definition of an 'urgent reason':

circumstances of such a nature that the terminating party cannot reasonably be required to continue the agreement, not even temporarily.

If the agreement is terminated for urgent reasons for which the other party is to blame, this other party will be liable for damages. A clause which leaves the decision about the 'urgency' of the reason to one of the parties, is void.

Termination by the court

The Cantonal Court may terminate the agreement at either party's request on the grounds of:

(1) circumstances considered as 'urgent reasons' (see above); the court will award compensation either to the agent or to the principal if the other party is to blame for such circumstances;

(2) a change in circumstances of such a nature that the agreement should reasonably be terminated at once or within a short period; the court may award compensation either to the agent or to the principal. There is no appeal from decisions of the Cantonal Court.

Compensation

In case of termination for 'urgent reasons' by either party or by the court, compensation as referred to can be claimed in the form of an amount equal to the commission which would have been earned during the notice period—an amount which may be mitigated by the court—or in the form of complete compensation for damages incurred, in which case the claimant will have to prove the extent of such damages.

Restraint of trade clause

A restraint of trade clause is only valid if it is in writing and if it relates to the kind of products and/or services, territory and group of customers covered by the agency.

The principal cannot invoke a restraint of trade clause:

(1) if the principal has terminated the agreement without consent of the agent without observance of the legal or agreed term and without an 'urgent reason', immediately notified to the agent;

(2) if the agent has terminated the agreement for an 'urgent reason', immediately notified to the principal, for which the principal is to blame;

(3) if the court has terminated the agreement based on circumstances for which the principal is to blame.

The Cantonal Courts can mitigate or completely set aside the restraint of trade clause. The court may also mitigate any contractual penalties due in case of violation of the restraint of trade clause.

Special protection of agent's commission

The following provisions are partly mandatory in the sense that they may not be deviated from to the detriment of the *agent*:

(1)　if a stipulation has been made that the agent is only entitled to his commission if the third party has performed the contract, then commission becomes due at the latest when the third party has executed his part of the transaction or should have done so if the principal had executed his part of the transaction;

(2)　the commission becomes payable at the latest on the date on which the written statement containing the commission due must be provided.

Goodwill indemnity

The following article may not be deviated from to the detriment of the agent before the end of the agreement.

Without prejudice to his right to claim damages, the agent is entitled to an indemnity at the end of the agency contract to the extent that:

(1)　he has increased the number of customers or has considerably increased the volume of contracts with the existing customers and the contracts with these customers still provide the principal with considerable benefits; and

(2)　payment of this indemnity is reasonable, taking into account all circumstances, in particular the commission *lost* on the contracts with these customers.

The amount of the indemnity does not exceed the remuneration of the agent of one year, calculated on the basis of the average annual remuneration over the last five years or, if the agency contract has lasted a shorter period, over the entire period in question.

The indemnity must be claimed by the agent within one year after the end of the agreement. The indemnity is not due if the agreement is terminated:

(1)　by the principal for an 'urgent reason' for which the agent is responsible;

(2)　by the agent unless for reasons attributable to the principal or for justified reasons such as age or illness of the agent;

(3)　by the agent which, in accordance with arrangements made with the principal, assigns his rights and obligations under the agreement to a third party.

7.4 DISTRIBUTION

7.4.1 NO SPECIFIC RULES

The Civil Code and Commercial Code do not contain specific provisions with respect to distribution other than in connection with the provisions on sale and purchase of goods.

Distribution is a vague term which comprises different forms of selling products or providing services at different levels.

7.4.2 EXCLUSIVE DISTRIBUTION

A foreign company may grant the exclusive distribution rights for the Netherlands to a Dutch company. As stated above, Dutch law does not contain specific provisions for such an agreement. However, the distribution agreement has to be in conformity with the EC Block Exemption 1983/83 (Official Journal 1983 L173/1) to avoid the risk of violation of art 85, para 1 of the EC Treaty.

Dutch law does not provide for an indemnification for *goodwill* built up by the distributor during the term of the agreement. If no term or period of notice has been agreed, 'reasonableness and fairness' will determine under what circumstances a distribution agreement may be terminated and what notice period must be observed.

Dutch law accepts the possibility of retention of title until the products to be delivered have been paid for. If the distributor is allowed to use the principal's *tradename*, it is advisable to make specific arrangements with respect to the tradename upon termination. This is necessary because the (Dutch) right to a tradename in principle belongs to the company who uses such a name in the Netherlands first.

Finally, it is important for the principal to have a specific provision in the distribution agreement on *bankruptcy* or a moratorium of payment of the distributor, because if no special provisions have been made such events are not in themselves reasons for termination.

7.4.3 SELECTIVE DISTRIBUTION

This form of distribution, in which the dealers can only sell to end-customers or to other dealers which are admitted to the distribution network, is allowed under Dutch law, but its compatibility with art 85, para 1 of the EC Treaty is doubtful in so far as products are concerned which are not technically complicated.

In practice, it is difficult to take action—on the basis of tort—against an outsider who sells the products which are selectively distributed. Apart from the question of whether selective distribution is allowed, it is up to the selective distributor to prove that his distribution network is completely closed, which means that it is not possible for an outsider to obtain products without somebody having breached his agreement with the selective distributor.

7.4.4 GENERAL CONDITIONS

General

Very often distributors of products or services use general conditions. Since 1 January 1992 the Civil Code contains specific provisions with respect to general conditions. As regards general conditions which were already in use before 1 January 1992 these provisions will become applicable as from 1 January 1993.

Definition

General conditions are defined as one or more written provisions which have been drafted in order to become part of a number of agreements with the exception of 'essential provisions'. Essential provisions are, in general, provisions without which it is not possible to reach a valid agreement, for instance on price and quantity of the goods.

When applicable

General conditions become part of an agreement if the other party has explicitly accepted the applicability or if he has given the user of the general conditions justified reason to believe that he has accepted the applicability. In general, it is not sufficient to send the text of the general conditions together with an order acceptance, except if the other party clearly indicates that he accepts such general conditions. For the applicability, general acceptance is sufficient. It is not necessary that the other party has agreed to each and every provision. Even the fact that the user of the general conditions knows that the other party was not aware of certain provisions does not exclude their applicability.

Invalidity

A provision in general conditions can be nullified when:

(1)   it is unreasonably burdensome;

(2)   the user did not give the other party a reasonable possibility to become aware of the contents of the general conditions. In general, a user has the obligation to send the text of the general conditions before the conclusion of the agreement or, if that is not possible (for instance an agreement concluded by telephone), to inform the other party before the conclusion of the agreement where the general conditions can be inspected while at the same time offering to send a copy and, if requested, to indeed send a copy. A copy does not have to be sent if it would be unreasonable to ask for it (for instance because of the extensiveness of the text).

The following parties cannot nullify general conditions on the grounds set out above:

(1)   large companies with more than 50 employees;

(2)   parties who themselves use such general conditions.

Unreasonably burdensome

'Unreasonably burdensomeness' of a certain provision in general conditions has to be proven by the party claiming it and should be judged on the basis of the specific circumstances in which such provision is invoked.

However, if general conditions are used in agreements with private consumers one should look at the so-called 'black' and 'grey' lists. The black list contains provisions which are always deemed to be unreasonably burdensome. The grey list contains provisions which are assumed to be unreasonably burdensome. However, the user of the general conditions has the right to prove that under the specific circumstances a provision which appears on the grey list is not unreasonably burdensome.

7.5 LICENSING

General

Dutch law only contains a few specific provisions relating to licensing. The general principles of the law of contract also apply to licence agreements. In practice, EC law and especially the Block Exemption of 30 November 1988 (Official Journal 1989 L61/1) for patent licence agreements and the Block Exemption of 23 July 1984 (Official Journal 1984 L219/15) for know-how licence agreements contain the most important provisions to be considered before entering into a licence agreement. The specific provisions in Dutch law are the following.

Patent law

As an agreement in general only gives rights against the infringing party, it is of great importance to file a patent licence agreement with the Patent Office. This results in the certainty that if the patent is assigned to another party (even after bankruptcy of the licensor) the licence remains in force.

A licensee does not have the right to ask for injunctions. However, an exclusive licensee has the right to sue for damages if he has so agreed with the patentee. Even without a specific agreement, an exclusive licensee has the right to join the patentee in proceedings for damages and claim his own damages.

Trademarks and designs

The Benelux Trademark Act and the Benelux Design Act contain the same provisions with respect to licence agreements.

In writing

A licence agreement with respect to a trademark or a design which is not in writing is null and void.

Restrictions

Restrictions in a trademark or design licence agreement other than with respect to the period for which the licence is granted, or in the case of trademark licence in respect of certain of the products (or services) for which the trademark has been registered can only be maintained by invoking the contractual rights under the licence agreement. This means that if a licensee who has obtained a licence for Belgium sells products under the licensed trademark in the Netherlands, the sale is not an infringement of the trademark rights, but only a violation of the licence agreement. Consequently, products thus sold in the Netherlands can circulate freely in the Netherlands, as the subsequent selling of such products cannot constitute a trademark infringement either.

Effect on third parties

The registration of (an excerpt of) the trademark or design licence agreement with the Benelux Trademark or Design Office is necessary in order to be able to invoke the agreement against third parties. This is, for instance, of importance in case of a transfer of the trademark to make sure that the licence is not lost and in case of a claim for damages by the licensee against an infringer.

Damages

A trademark or design licensee has the right to claim compensation for the damages suffered as a result of an infringement if he acts together with the owner of the trademark or design. As the licensee does not have the right to claim such damages on his own, it is wise for the licensee to include a provision in the licence agreement which obliges the trademark or design owner to join him in proceedings for damages.

7.6 FRANCHISING

Dutch law does not contain any specific provision with respect to franchise agreements. As far as the franchise includes a trademark or patent licence, the specific provision to trademark and patent licences will be applicable. With respect to trade-names, reference is made to section **6.6**.

There is some case law in the Netherlands which protects the specific interior of for instance a shop. The right to use such specific interior ('get up') can therefore be included in the franchise.

The most important provisions with respect to franchise agreements can be found in EC law and especially in the 1988 Block Exception for franchise agreements of 30 November 1988 (Official Journal 1988 L 359/47).

8
INSOLVENCY

8.1 INTRODUCTION

Bankruptcy and moratorium of payment

If a person (including a legal entity) is unable to pay his debts, Dutch law provides for two special regimes:

(1) bankruptcy (*faillissement*); and
(2) moratorium of payment (*surséance van betaling*).

In general, moratorium of payment will be granted if it is expected that the person will become able to pay his debts after a certain period of time or pursuant to a composition with the creditors while bankruptcy will be declared if there is no such expectation.

The main source of Dutch insolvency law is the Bankruptcy Act (*Faillissementswet*) of 1893 as amended. The latest amendment is the amendment of 1 January 1992.

8.2 INTERNATIONAL ASPECTS

Foreign bankruptcy

In respect of foreign bankrupties, Dutch insolvency law has adopted the principle of territoriality. This means that a foreign bankruptcy in principle has no effect in the Netherlands. Assets located in the Netherlands belonging to a person who has been declared bankrupt outside the Netherlands are not considered part of the bankrupt estate. From the point of view of Dutch law, creditors may, in principle, seize such assets as a security for their claims or execute judgements against such assets (to the extent that such execution is possible in the Netherlands). The bankrupt person can also be declared bankrupt in the Netherlands.

Notwithstanding the foregoing, the receiver in a foreign bankruptcy can act in Dutch proceedings for instance to recover a claim belonging to the bankrupt person. Assets which belonged to the bankrupt estate and which were, at the time of the bankruptcy, situated in the country where the person was declared bankrupt, will remain part of the bankrupt estate if they are moved to the Netherlands by the receiver. A receiver in a foreign bankruptcy can therefore sell goods belonging to the estate to a purchaser in the Netherlands without having to fear that creditors in the Netherlands will seize such goods or, for that matter, the monies owed by the purchaser in the Netherlands.

Dutch bankruptcy

In respect of Dutch bankruptcies, the prevailing view is that the principle of universality is adhered to. Obviously, this principle is limited by the concept of sovereignty, but according to the Supreme Court it has not been the intention of the Bankruptcy Act to limit the effect of a Dutch bankruptcy to the assets located in the Netherlands.

The following can be seen as an elaboration of the principle of universality in the Bankruptcy Act and in case law.

The Bankruptcy Act obliges creditors who seek recourse against foreign assets of the bankrupt, to pay to the bankrupt estate the amount for which they have thus sought recourse. In practice, this could mean that a foreign creditor who obtains payment from a Dutch bankrupt company by execution of its foreign assets may be confronted with a claim of the receiver who could enforce such a claim against the assets of the foreign creditor that are located in the Netherlands.

The Dutch Supreme Court has further decided that also an action performed abroad by a Dutch bankrupt company can be invalidated on the grounds set out in the Bankruptcy Act and that the receiver is entitled to recover foreign assets to the extent he is able to do so under the foreign local law.

On the basis of the Statute for the Kingdom of the Netherlands a Dutch bankruptcy also has effect in the Netherlands Antilles and Aruba and *vice versa*. Local statutory provisions must be complied with.

Treaties

Application of the principle of universality is enhanced by treaties. According to the Netherlands–Belgian Execution Treaty of 1925 a Belgian bankruptcy has effect in the Netherlands and a Dutch bankruptcy has effect in Belgium. Reference should also be made to the Netherlands–German Execution Treaty of 1962, on the basis of which certain limited measures in bankruptcy and moratorium may be recognised and enforced.

A draft EC Convention concerning bankruptcy, creditors' arrangements and similar proceedings, has already been the subject of discussions for many years.

The Committee of Ministers of the Council of Europe adopted a convention on certain international aspects of bankruptcy in February 1990. This convention is not yet in force for the Netherlands.

8.3   SECURITY AND INSOLVENCY

Security rights

Bankruptcy and moratorium of payment in general do not affect the rights of secured creditors. Mortgage, pledge, fiduciary ownership and retention of title are in general not affected and can be exercised (provided this takes place timely) separately from the bankruptcy.

Priority

Dutch law grants priority to certain claims. This can be a priority with respect to all the assets of the bankrupt estate or with respect to certain goods. A moratorium of payment does not affect the right of a preferred creditor to exercise his priority—but only in respect of the assets to which the priority relates—and have the debtor pay his debt. If the priority relates to certain assets only, the moratorium of payment continues to have effect in respect of the other assets.

Retention of title

Certain creditors have the right to retain goods owed by the debtor until he pays his debts. Such retention rights are not affected by bankruptcy or moratorium of payment and these creditors do not have to return the relevant goods to the bankrupt estate as long as they are not paid in full.

After 1 January 1992

Since 1 January 1992 it is impossible to obtain a valid right of fiduciary ownership. However, the law with respect to pledge has changed to make it possible to pledge goods while the debtor keeps the goods in his possession.

Under the present rules it is also possible to pledge claims without having to inform the debtor. Future claims can only be pledged to the extent that they result from a legal relation that exists at the time of the pledge. Such pledge can only be invoked against the receiver or administrator if the claims actually existed at the time of the bankruptcy or moratorium of payment.

Retention of title remains possible.

One of the most important changes is the introduction of what is sometimes referred to as the 'cool-down' period. Under the amended Bankruptcy Act the Supervisory Judge may, at the request of any interested party or *ex officio* decide that, during a maximum period of one month, third parties may only seek recourse against the assets belonging to the bankrupt estate or claim goods in the bankrupt person's possession, after having obtained authorisation from the Supervisory Judge to do so. The 'cool-down' period may be extended once by a maximum of one month.

This provision intends to grant the receiver some time to take decisions on how to administer the bankruptcy, to see what rights third parties have in respect of goods which are in the possession of the bankrupt person (are these goods part of the bankrupt estate?) and what goods should be preserved for the estate (eg in connection with continuation of an enterprise).

8.4   BANKRUPTCY

8.4.1   INTRODUCTION

General seizure

Bankruptcy is a general statutory seizure of the assets of the debtor followed by liquidation for the benefit of the creditors. Such liquidation will not take place if there are no or hardly any assets or if a composition with the creditors is reached.

Bankruptcy of a company and subsequent liquidation of the company's assets result in the dissolution of the company.

8.4.2 DECLARATION OF BANKRUPTCY

Having ceased to pay debts

A debtor who has ceased to pay his debts can be declared bankrupt. A request to the competent district court can be made by:

(1) the debtor himself;

(2) one or more creditors; or

(3) the Public Prosecutor (because of reasons of public interest).

Proceedings; appeals

The request has to state facts and circumstances that constitute *prima facie* evidence that the debtor has ceased to pay his debts. This is considered to be the case if there are at least two creditors, one of whom has a claim which is due and payable and which the debtor refuses to pay.

The court will in principle hear the debtor but has to handle the request with dispatch. If the debtor has not been heard, he has the right to ask for a review by the same court within 14 days. Creditors (except the creditor who has filed the request) and interested parties have the same right but have to exercise it within eight days.

Appeals to the Court of Appeal and thereafter to the Supreme Court can be lodged by the debtor and by the creditors or interested parties against a judgement pronouncing or refusing to pronounce bankruptcy.

Such appeals have to be lodged within eight days following the appealed decision.

8.4.3 THE ADMINISTRATION OF THE BANKRUPTCY; APPOINTMENT OF SUPERVISORY JUDGE AND RECEIVER(S)

Supervisory judge; receiver

The bankruptcy judgement contains appointment of a judge (*rechter-commissaris*) in charge with the supervision of the bank-ruptcy and the appointment of one or more receivers who are entrusted with the administration of the bankruptcy. For certain decisions the receiver needs the approval of the supervisory judge. Creditors and the bankrupt debtor can, by written request, appeal against each act of the receiver and/or ask the supervisory judge to order the receiver to act in a certain way. From a decision of the supervisory judge, appeal to the District Court is possible within five days after the decision.

In general, the court appoints members of the bar (advocates) as receivers.

Receiver's role

The receiver is entrusted with the administration of the bankrupt estate. He has to act in the best interest of the creditors. In his capacity of receiver he has the right to enter into agreements. The party that becomes creditor as a result of such an agreement in principle has a direct full claim against the bankrupt estate. The receiver has the right to continue the business of a bankrupt company.

Every three months the receiver has to file a report on the status of the bankruptcy. This report is deposited with the court and is open for inspection by the public.

The salary of the receiver is determined by the court.

8.4.4   THE CONSEQUENCES OF BANKRUPTCY

Legal capacity

From the day the bankruptcy is declared the bankrupt debtor loses his right to administer and dispose of his assets. The estate will not be responsible for any obligations of the debtor which have come into existence after the day of the bankruptcy unless (and to the extent that) the estate has benefited.

Court proceedings

The receiver replaces the debtor in pending or new court proceedings concerning the assets and liabilities of the debtor, of course in so far as they relate to the bankrupt estate. If the receiver refuses to replace the debtor in a case in which the debtor was the plaintiff, the defendant can ask the court to strike out the case.

Creditors cannot initiate court proceedings with respect to obligations of the debtor, again in so far as these obligations relate to the bankrupt estate. Claims resulting from such obligations have to be filed for verification (see section **8.4.5**).

If the receiver refuses to replace the debtor as defendant in a court case, the subsequent decision against the debtor results in a valid claim in the bankruptcy.

Agreements

In principle, a bankruptcy does not change the validity or the contents of an agreement. However, the obligation of the receiver to perform under an agreement may conflict with his duty to treat all non-privileged creditors as equal. In such cases of conflict the receiver does not have the obligation to perform and the other party will have to settle for monetary damages, a claim for which must be filed for verification.

The Bankruptcy Act contains specific provisions with respect to certain types of agreements. If an agreement contains rights and obligations for both parties and none of them has completely fulfilled his obligations, the non-bankrupt party may request the receiver to declare within eight days that he will perform under the agreement. If no such declaration is given, the agreement is dissolved and the non-bankrupt party will have the right to file his claim for damages for verification. If the receiver does give the requested declaration, he will have to put up security for the performance of his obligations.

Further specific provisions deal with—*inter alia*—hire purchase, tenancy and employment agreements (for employment agreements see Chapter 3).

'Pauliana'

The Bankruptcy Act contains several provisions which invalidate acts of the debtor carried out before the bankruptcy which are detrimental to the creditors.

In the first place the nullity can be invoked of all *voluntary* acts by the debtor, the results of which are detrimental to the creditors if both the debtor and his counter party knew that such acts would have a detrimental consequence.

With respect to certain voluntary acts carried out during the year preceding the bankruptcy to which the debtor had not committed himself before that period, knowledge of detrimental consequence is assumed for both debtor and his counter party, unless the contrary is proved. This is for instance the case:

(1) for a transaction in which the value of the performance by the debtor by far exceeds the value of the performance by his counter party;

(2) if the debtor pays a debt or gives security for a debt which is not yet due; or

(3)   if the debtor is a company and has entered into a transaction with a group company.

In case of gifts, only the debtor needs to have knowledge of the detrimental consequences for creditors in order to make it possible to invalidate such gifts. For gifts made within one year before the bankruptcy, such knowledge is again assumed unless the contrary is proved.

Obligatory acts

In the second place, acts to which the debtor was obliged can, under certain circumstances, be invalidated. Payment to a creditor who knew that the request for bankruptcy was pending can be invalidated. The same applies to the payment of a debt pursuant to consultation between the debtor and the creditor where the consultation was intended to put the creditor in a more favourable position than the other creditors.

Set-off

Claims against the debtor in existence at the time of the bankruptcy or resulting from agreements with the debtor entered into before the bankruptcy can be set-off against claims held by the debtor that meet the same requirements. If such claims are conditional or if the value is not certain, then the value on the date of the bankruptcy will be estimated. However, claims due within a year of the bankruptcy can be used for set-off against the full amount.

A claim against the debtor which has been assigned by a third party before the bankruptcy can only be used for set-off by the assignee if the assignee acted in good faith at the time of the assignment. If the assignee had reasons to believe that a bankruptcy was forthcoming he will not be considered to have acted in good faith. Claims assigned by a third party after the bankruptcy has been declared can never be used for set-off.

8.4.5   VERIFICATION

General

In principle, not later than 14 days after the judgement by which the debtor has been declared bankrupt becomes final, the supervisory judge determines the day on which claims against the bankrupt estate have to be filed and the date on which the verification meeting will take place. However, in practice, such a meeting is only called if this seems necessary.

Acknowledgement; dispute

The receiver communicates the dates by letter to all known creditors and will further make an announcement in a newspaper or newspapers designated by the supervisory judge. Each creditor will have to file his claim (and—if applicable—priority) with the receiver together with evidence of the existence of the claim. If the receiver acknowledges a claim it is put on the list of preliminary accepted claims. If he disputes the claim, he will contact the creditor giving reasons. If such contact with the creditor is not followed by acknowledgement, the receiver will put the claim on the list of disputed claims.

Verification meeting

During the verification meeting of creditors which takes place under the presidency of the supervisory judge, creditors and debtor can dispute the acceptance or priority of preliminary accepted claims and the supervisory judge will try to reconcile the disputed claims.

Claims accepted during that meeting become definitive. Claims which remain disputed will be dealt with by the court which decides whether such claims have to be accepted.

8.4.6 LIQUIDATION OF THE BANKRUPT ESTATE

General

If no composition with the creditors is reached (see section 8.6) the bankrupt estate will be liquidated for the benefit of the creditors after the verification meeting of the creditors.

Liquidation will take place by sale of the assets in a public sale or, with the approval of the supervisory judge, in a private sale.

Distribution of proceeds

After having paid the debts of the estate, which result either from his acts as receiver or are defined by law as estate debts and after having obtained all that was owed to the debtor, the receiver will distribute the proceeds amongst the creditors whose claims have been accepted, taking into consideration the different acknowledged priority rights. In large bankruptcies it is not unusual that there are one or more intermediate distributions of proceeds. Because of the many priorities (tax and social security payments at present still have top priority) and the usually large number of secured debts, it is very rare that distribution of proceeds amongst the non-privileged creditors takes place.

8.5   MORATORIUM OF PAYMENT

8.5.1   PURPOSE

A moratorium of payments is a suspension of the obligation to pay debts. The purpose is to prevent bankruptcy of a debtor who is unable to pay but who may be able to pay in the future. In such cases a bankruptcy would lead to an erosion of capital value which is not in the interest of the creditors.

8.5.2   THE GRANTING OF A MORATORIUM OF PAYMENT

General

A debtor who foresees that he will be unable to pay all his due debts may request the court to grant a moratorium of payment. The court will grant a temporary moratorium of payment upon receipt of the request and will appoint a supervisory judge and one or more administrators. The decision with respect to a definitive moratorium of payment will be made after a court hearing during which the supervisory judge, the administrator and the creditors will be heard.

Grounds to refuse a moratorium

The court can refuse a definitive moratorium on any ground it sees fit. However, the Bankruptcy Act sets out three grounds which oblige the court to refuse a definitive moratorium:

(1)   creditors representing more than one-quarter of the debtors represented at the hearing or representing more than one-third of all outstanding debts vote against a moratorium of payment;

(2)   there is reasonable fear that the debtor will try to prejudice the creditors during the moratorium of payment;

(3)   there is no prospect that the debtor will be able to pay his

creditors after a certain period of time or that he will be able to offer a composition.

Appeals and maximum duration

From the judgement of the District Court appeal is possible to the Court of Appeal and thereafter to the Supreme Court. Pending appeals, the moratorium remains in force.

The moratorium of payment can be granted for a maximum period of a year and a half with the possibility of one or more extensions for the same maximum period.

8.5.3 THE ADMINISTRATOR

The difference between a bankrupt debtor and a debtor who has obtained a moratorium of payment is that the latter does not lose the disposition and administration of his property as a result of the judgement. The restriction for a debtor in moratorium of payment is that he is not allowed to manage his business (concerning his disposition and administration) without the cooperation, the authorisation or the assistance of the administrator.

The Bankruptcy Act provides that the debtor's property is not liable if contracts have been entered into without the cooperation, the authorisation or the assistance of the administrator.

A receiver in a bankruptcy 'replaces' the bankrupt debtor but an administrator does not replace the debtor; administrator and debtor are like 'Siamese twins' during the moratorium of payment. In principle, the one cannot act without the other.

Every three months the administrator in a moratorium of payment has to make a report of the situation of the debtor's property which report will be filed with the court and is open for inspection by the public.

8.5.4 THE CONSEQUENCE OF A MORATORIUM OF PAYMENT

No obligation to pay

The most important consequence of a moratorium of payment is that the debtor's obligation to pay his non-privileged and unsecured debts is suspended. Also, attachments of assets levied by creditors to ensure payment of their debts lapse as soon as the decision granting a definitive moratorium of payment or approving a composition with creditors has become final, unless the District Court, at the request of the administrator, determines an earlier date for lapse of attachment. Court cases involving the non-payment of debts by the debtor will be suspended.

Debts incurred before the moratorium can only be paid with the approval of the administrator and in such a case all creditors have to be paid in proportion of their claims.

However, it should be noted that holders of mortgages, pledges and also priority rights can exercise their rights.

Debts incurred after the granting ot the moratorium of payment with the approval, or on the basis of authorisation, of the administrator are not affected by the moratorium and have to be paid in full.

Court cases

With the exception of court cases involving the payment of monies owed by the debtor at the time the moratorium was granted, pending court proceedings will continue and new court proceedings can be initiated.

Agreements

The same rules apply as in the case of bankruptcy (see section **8.4.4**).

8.5.5   TERMINATION OF THE MORATORIUM

The moratorium can be terminated by the court *ex officio* or at the request of the administrator or one or more creditors, for instance if the debtor is acting against the interest of the creditors or if there is no expectation that the debtor will be able to pay his creditors in the future.

In such a situation the court will normally declare the debtor bankrupt.

The moratorium can also be terminated at the request of the debtor after the administrator and creditors have been heard if the debtor is capable again of paying his debts.

Finally, a moratorium may be terminated because of a composition reached between the debtor and his creditors.

8.6 COMPOSITION WITH CREDITORS

8.6.1 INTRODUCTION

In theory, a debtor can offer a composition to his creditors without being in bankruptcy or having been granted a moratorium of payment. In practice, the problem in reaching such a composition lies in the fact that no creditor can be forced to accept the composition against his wishes. This is different if the debtor is in bankruptcy or has been granted a moratorium of payment. The Bankruptcy Act contains provisions for both situations which make it possible to give the composition binding force also *vis-à-vis* creditors who are against such composition.

The advantage of a composition is clear. The debtor is liberated from the remainder of his debts.

There are no rules for the contents of a composition. Usually the debtor (or receiver or administrator as the case may be) offers his creditors with non-privileged claims a specific percentage of their claims. Sometimes there is a full payment of claims that do not exceed a specific amount and partial payment of claims exceeding that amount. Composition only binds non-privileged creditors. On a voluntary basis, composition-like arrangements can also be made with privileged creditors. An offer may also amount to an extension of payment or payment in instalments.

8.6.2 BANKRUPTCY AND MORATORIUM OF PAYMENT

In order to give a composition binding force, two-thirds of the non-privileged creditors representing at least three-quarters of the non-privileged claims which have been (preliminarily) admitted, have to vote in favour of the composition.

The court has to approve the composition. The court will refuse approval—*inter alia*—if it is of the opinion that the assets of the debtor are clearly insufficient for the payment of the composition. After the decision of the court to approve the composition has become final, all non-privileged creditors are bound to the composition.

Appeals against the decision of the court can be lodged with the Court of Appeal and thereafter with the Supreme Court.

LEGISLATION TABLE

INDEX

242 *Index*